物流服务与管理专业新形态一体化系列教材

国际货代英语

- 主　编　陆佳宜　孙　丽
- 副主编　赵琳娟　李吉龙
- 参　编　吴婧斐　沈炜娜　傅哲莹
　　　　　毛月滢　何　萍

北京理工大学出版社
BEIJING INSTITUTE OF TECHNOLOGY PRESS

版权专有　侵权必究

图书在版编目（CIP）数据

国际货代英语 / 陆佳宜，孙丽主编.--北京：北京理工大学出版社，2022.4
　　ISBN 978-7-5763-1164-8

Ⅰ.①国… Ⅱ.①陆…②孙… Ⅲ.①国际货运—货运代理—英语—中等专业学校—教材　Ⅳ.①F511.41

中国版本图书馆CIP数据核字（2022）第045678号

出版发行 / 北京理工大学出版社有限责任公司	
社　　址 / 北京市海淀区中关村南大街5号	
邮　　编 / 100081	
电　　话 /（010）68914775（总编室）	
（010）82562903（教材售后服务热线）	
（010）68944723（其他图书服务热线）	
网　　址 / http://www.bitpress.com.cn	
经　　销 / 全国各地新华书店	
印　　刷 / 定州市新华印刷有限公司	
开　　本 / 889毫米×1194毫米　1/16	
印　　张 / 10.5	责任编辑 / 武丽娟
字　　数 / 204千字	文案编辑 / 武丽娟
版　　次 / 2022年4月第1版　2022年4月第1次印刷	责任校对 / 刘亚男
定　　价 / 40.00元	责任印制 / 边心超

图书出现印装质量问题，请拨打售后服务热线，本社负责调换

前言

"国际货代英语"是中等职业学校国际货代专业的专业核心课。本教材贯彻"做中学，学中做"的教学理念，以国际货代英语工作能力为中心，在新制定的中职国际货代专业国家课标的指导下，设置学习单元的职业能力和素质、知识、能力要求，依照国际货代业务关键环节的活动场景来设计教学模块、教学项目和教学任务，以工作流程为导向，把物流的英语专业词汇和相关典型句型结合到任务的实施过程中去，使学生能沉浸在典型情境中应用英语，在实践中先学习再应用，从应用中发现问题，再学习和提升货代英语应用能力。

本教材分为销售、海运、空运和售后服务四大模块，货代销售、货代合同、海运报价、海运操作、空运报价、空运操作、客户异议和客户索赔八个项目，常见沟通方式、货代公司业务介绍、认识出口货代合同、认识进口货代合同、海运电话报价、海运邮件报价、认识海运主要港口/航线/公司、阅读海运操作函电、空运电话报价、空运邮件报价、认识空运主要港口/航线/公司、阅读空运信函、认识常见客户异议、沟通客户异议、认识货运保险费率、沟通保险索赔十六个任务。

每一任务由任务

PREFACE

导入、任务实施、知识检测三个环节组成。第一环节为任务导入，即任务的布置环节，提出模拟国际货代企业实务工作的背景材料。第二环节为任务实施：学生首先自主学习或在教师引导下，在知识学苑中，学习这一环节需要的知识、词汇、句型；通过两到四个循序渐进、逐级提升的环节，采用各种学生喜闻乐见的教学形式，完成对于词汇、句型的巩固和阅读、写作、口语表达能力的训练，最终在语言实践中完成该任务。最后一个环节为知识检测，发挥学生的主体性，自主对之前所学的词汇、句型和任务完成情况进行自我检测。

本课程拟上144学时，具体学时分配如下。

模块	项目	任务	学时分配
模块一 销售	项目一 货代销售	任务一 常见沟通方式	6
		任务二 货代公司业务介绍	10
	项目二 货代合同	任务一 认识出口货代合同	10
		任务二 认识进口货代合同	10
模块二 海运	项目一 海运报价	任务一 海运电话报价	12
		任务二 海运邮件报价	8
	项目二 海运操作	任务一 认识海运主要港口/航线/公司	8
		任务二 阅读海运操作函电	12
模块三 空运	项目一 空运报价	任务一 空运电话报价	12
		任务二 空运邮件报价	8
	项目二 空运操作	任务一 认识空运主要港口/航线/公司	8
		任务二 阅读空运信函	12
模块四 售后服务	项目一 客户异议	任务一 认识常见客户异议	4
		任务二 沟通客户异议	8
	项目二 客户索赔	任务一 认识货运保险费率	6
		任务二 沟通保险索赔	10
		合计	144

PREFACE

　　本书由浙江省杭州市财经职业学校陆佳宜老师、孙丽老师任主编，具体编写分工如下：浙江省杭州市萧山区第三中等职业学校沈炜娜老师编写模块一项目一，浙江省杭州市财经职业学校赵琳娟老师编写模块一项目二任务一和模块二项目二，陆佳宜老师编写模块二项目一，浙江省杭州市财经职业学校吴婧斐老师编写模块三项目一，浙江省杭州市财经职业学校李吉龙老师编写模块一项目二任务二和模块三项目二，浙江省杭州第二中学傅哲莹老师和孙丽老师共同编写模块四项目一，浙江省桐庐县职业技术学校毛月滢老师编写模块四项目二。全书由陆佳宜老师和孙丽老师编制样章、统稿、修改并最后定稿，赵琳娟老师对于英语部分进行校对。北京络捷斯特科技发展股份有限公司市场总监何萍参与编写和指导，提供了部分资料和修改建议。

　　本书在编写过程中参阅了许多相关教材，吸收、引用了大量有关资源，谨在此一并致以诚挚的谢意！

　　由于编者水平有限，书中难免存在不足之处，恳请同行、专家和广大读者不吝指正。

编　者

目 录
CONTENTS

Module One　　Marketing ··· 1

模块一　销售 ··· 1

  Project One　　Forwarder Sales ·· 2

  项目一　货代销售 ·· 2

  Project Two　　Shipping Agency Agreement ··· 23

  项目二　货代合同 ·· 23

Module Two　　Marine Freight Transport ·· 49

模块二　海运 ··· 49

  Project One　　Sea Quotations ·· 50

  项目一　海运报价 ·· 50

  Project Two　　Sea Freight Operation ·· 70

  项目二　海运操作 ·· 70

Module Three　　Air Freight Transport ·· 89

模块三　空运 ··· 89

  Project One　　Air Quotations ··· 90

  项目一　空运报价 ·· 90

Project Two　Air Freight Operation 107

项目二　空运操作 107

Module Four　After-sale Service 125
模块四　售后服务 125

Project One　Customer Complaint 126

项目一　客户异议 126

Project Two　Customer Claims 143

项目二　客户索赔 143

Module One　Marketing
模块一　销　售

项目一
货代销售
Project One　Forwarder Sales

【学习目标】

1. 能描述货代销售过程中常见的沟通方式。
2. 能读懂公司货代业务的简介，并撰写相关公司的货代业务介绍。
3. 在学习货代销售的过程中，根据商务礼仪规范，展现良好企业形象。

Task One　Common Means of Communication
任务一　常见沟通方式

【任务导入】

小陈是上海前进国际货代公司的实习销售人员，现公司对新进的实习员工进行统一培训，培训内容主要是常见的货代业务沟通方式，常见的有与客户面对面交流，与客户电话交流和电子邮件沟通这三种。作为一名实习销售人员，小陈决定做一个合格的销售员，先规范、顺畅地用专业语言与客户沟通，充分展现企业的良好形象，为公司争取更多的业务量。

请跟随小陈一起学习货代公司中常见的沟通方式吧！

【任务实施】

一、学习描述货代公司性质的常见词汇

请先进入知识学苑（1-1-1）开展任务实施前的学习，认识常见的描述货代公司性质的典型词汇。

知识学苑（1-1-1）——常见的描述货代公司性质的典型词汇

1. Container Freight Forwarding——集装箱货运代理
2. State-owned Enterprise——国有企业
3. International Air Transport Association（IATA）——国际航空运输协会
4. International Federation Of Freight Forwarders Associations（FIATA）——国际货运代理协会
5. Licensed Offices——有执照的办事处
6. Third Party Logistics（3PL）——第三方物流
7. Freight Forwarding Company——货运代理公司
8. Logistics Company——物流公司
9. Import /Export Manager——进 / 出口经理

（一）Think and Match 读词汇，匹配词汇名称

在"知识学苑"中学习了常见描述货代公司性质的典型词汇，小陈认识了一些有关货代公司的词汇，接下来公司将进行第一轮词汇考察，看下有多少实习生能灵活掌握有关货代公司性质的相关词汇。如图 1-1-1，请将英文表述与中文表述进行正确连线：

图 1-1-1　常见描述货代公司性质词汇

（二）Read and Conclusion 读短文，总结常见沟通方式

小陈在培训期间还学习了与客户进行沟通时常用的几种方式，现在请阅读下面短文，总结这些方式。

1. Read

There are three usual ways of communication with customers in the Freight forwarders, the first one is to talk on the phone, the second one is to talk face to face, and the third one is to communicate by mail.

The customer communication features are: ① The language should be polite, appropriate, short and concise. ② The language should be precise and specific. ③ The language needs to be formal and universal. ④ Language vocabulary should be specialized.

【参考译文】

货运代理通常的沟通方式有三种，第一种是与客户通电话，第二种是与客户面对面交谈，第三种是通过邮件与客户沟通。

货代公司与客户沟通时的特点有：①语言要礼貌、得体、简短精悍。②语言要准确、具体。③语言要正式规范，具有通用性。④语言词汇要专业化。

2. Conclusion

What are the common ways of communication in the sales of freight forwarders?

二、学习货代销售中电话沟通方式的表达句型

请先进入知识学苑（1-1-2）开展任务实施前的准备，学习常见电话沟通方式的表达句型。

> 知识学苑 (1-1-2)——常见电话沟通方式的表达句型
>
> 1. A: Hello! Is this ABC Freight Forwarding Company?
>   你好，是 ABC 货运代理公司吗？
>   B: Yes. What can I do for you?
>   是的，我们能为您做些什么？
> 2. A: May I speak to the export manager, please?
>   我能和出口经理沟通吗？
>   B: Speaking. What can I do for you?
>   我能为您做些什么？
>   A: This is Mark from ABC Internet Sale calling from Japan. We have learned that your company is one of the main exporters of Chinese silk（中国丝绸）.
>   我是 ABC 互联网销售公司的马克，从日本打来的电话。我们了解到您们是中国丝绸主要的出口商。
>   B: That's right. What can I do for you?
>   没错，我能为你做什么？
> 3. A: Hello! Is that DDD Clothing Company.
>   你好，是 DDD 服装公司吗？
>   B: Yes! Excuse me, but who's calling, please?
>   是的，不好意思，请问您是哪位？
>   A: I'm a customer service representative of ABC Freight Forwarding Company. I'm calling to inform you the goods information.
>   我是 ABC 货代公司的客户服务代表，我打这个电话是想告诉您货物信息。
> 4. This is what I should do! Goodbye!
>   这是我应该做的！再见！
> 5. I guarantee!
>   我保证。

（一）Choose and Judge 做选择，判断句型

1. Choose

小陈学习了常见的沟通表达句型后，进入培训考核的第二个阶段，那让我们跟着小陈一起读句型，选择恰当的语句，看看能否顺利通过第二轮考察。从每一题的 A、B 两种表述中，选择适合在常见沟通方式中采用的语句，在括号内打"√"。

（1）（   ）A. Hello! Who are you?
　　　（   ）B. Hello! Excuse me, but who's calling, please?

（2）（   ）A. Who's that, may I ask?
　　　（   ）B. Who are you?

（3）（   ）A. Hello! May I speak to the import manager, please?
　　　（   ）B. Hi! I want to speak to the Import Manager.

（4）（   ）A. This is what I shouldn't do! Goodbye!

模块一 销 售

（　　）B. This is what I should do! Goodbye!

（5）（　　）A. I guarantee!

（　　）B. I'm not sure!

2. Judge and Modify 判断和修改句型

通过以上的学习与训练，小陈尝试对下列对话中的不恰当语句进行判断与修改。请在括号内填"R/W"，若为错误语句，请将修改好的句子填写在横线上面，最后判断是属于"来电对话"还是"去电对话"。

（1）A: Hello! Is this QIANJIN freight forwarding company？

（　　）_____

B: Yes, who are you?

（　　）_____

A: I'm Mark, a manager of clothing company. My clothing was supposed to arrive two days ago. But the goods are still not sent to my company.

（　　）_____

_____

B: Really? First please let me check the goods information.

（　　）_____

这是_____（来电/去电对话）。

（2）A: Hello, is that HANGZHOU Electronic Technology Company?

（　　）_____

B: Yes! Excuse me, but who's calling, please?

（　　）_____

A: I'm QIANJIN freight forwarding company's customer service representative. I make this phone call to inform you that the goods have reached Tianjin Port. Next, you must listen to our advice.

（　　）_____

_____

B: Oh, it is so fast! So, what should we do?

（　　）_____

这是_____（来电/去电对话）。

三、学习货代销售中面对面沟通方式的表达句型

请先进入知识学苑（1-1-3）开展任务实施前的准备，学习常见面对面沟通方式的表达句型。

知识学苑（1-1-3）——常见面对面沟通方式的表达句型
1. Good morning, sir! It is a pleasure to meet you! 早上好，先生！很荣幸能认识您！ 2. A: Welcome to our company, Mark, nice to meet you! 欢迎来到我们公司，马克，很高兴见到你！ B: Nice to meet you! 很高兴见到你！ A: Mark, my name is Chen Fei. Here is my card. I would like to introduce our company. 马克，我的名字叫陈飞，这是我的名片。我将给你介绍我们的公司 B: Thanks a lot. 非常感谢。 3. A: Please don't hesitate to tell me if you have any questions. 如果你有什么问题，请尽管问我。 B: Thank you very much. 非常感谢。 A: If you are available, I'm hoping to meet you. 如果你有时间，我希望能拜访你。 4. If you have any questions, please feel free to contact me at any time. 如果你有任何问题，请随时与我们联系。 5. We hope to establish a long-term business relationship with you. 我们希望与你们建立业务关系。 6. I sincerely hope that we could establish a long-term relationship of cooperation. Thanks again for your interest. 我真诚地希望我们能建立长期的合作关系，再次感谢您的关注。

（一）Read and Translate 读对话，翻译对话句型

小陈为了提高自己的英语沟通业务能力，认真学习培训中的对话脚本，并尝试进行中英文互译。

（1）Mr. Chen: Good afternoon, Sir. It is a pleasure to meet you! What I can do for you?

中文：_____

Mr. Black: Good afternoon, I'd like to get to know your company.

中文：_____

Mr. Chen: 好的，我很荣幸能为您介绍我们的公司。

英文：_____

（2）Mr. Clinton: Hello! Is this Ningbo Haichang Freight Forwarding Company？

中文：_____

Mr. Chen: 是的，可以问下，您是谁吗？

英文：_____

Mr. Clinton: 我是克林顿，是英国一家服装公司的经理。We have learned that you are one of the best container freight forwarding companies in China.

中文：_____

英文：_____

Mr. Chen: 是的，很高兴能为您服务。

英文：_____

（3）I sincerely hope that we could establish a long-term cooperative relationship! Thanks again for your interest.

中文：_____

（二）Read and Judge 读对话，判断以下对话属于电话沟通方式还是面对面沟通方式，划出该沟通方式的典型句子

（1）第一段对话：

A: Hello! Is this ABC Freight Forwarding Company?

B: Yes, excuse me, but who's calling, please?

A: I'm a manager of a home appliance company.

B: What can I do for you, Sir?

A: Oh, actually we need a large amount of products to be shipped from Shanghai to London.

B: We hope to establish long-term business relationship with you.

这是_____沟通方式。

（2）第二段对话：

A: Welcome to our company, Andy, nice to meet you!

B: Nice to meet you!

A: Andy, my name is Xiao Chen. Here is my card. I would like to introduce our company.

B: Thanks a lot.

A: Our company was established in 2000. As a 3PL, we will provide you with the best logistics service.

这是_____沟通方式。

四、学习货代销售中电子邮件沟通方式的表达句型

请先进入知识学苑（1-1-4）开展任务实施前的准备，学习常见电子邮件沟通方式的表达句型。

知识学苑 (1-1-4)——常见电子邮件沟通方式的表达句型

1. Dear Mr./Mrs. Smith（信件开头）
亲爱的史密斯先生/女士
2. Thank you for choosing our company.（正文开头例句）
感谢您选择我们的公司。
3. I took the liberty of writing to you in order to establish business relationship.（正文开头例句）
我冒昧地写信给您，是为了能跟你们建立业务关系。
4. I took the liberty of writing to you about our company.（正文开头例句）
我冒昧写信告诉您我们公司的情况。
5. Please believe that we will provide the most professional freight forwarding services.（结束语例句）
请相信我们一定会提供最专业的货代服务。
6. Please feel free to contact us directly.（结束语例句）
请随时与我们联系。
7. We hope to receive your detailed inquiry soon.（结束语例句）
我们希望尽快收到您的详细均价。
8. We are looking forward to having the chance of cooperating with you in the near future.（结束语例句）
我们希望在不久的将来，能有机会与你们合作。
9. I sincerely hope that we could establish a long-term cooperative relationship! Thanks again for your interest.（结束语例句）
我真诚地期望我们能建立长期合作关系！感谢您的关注。
10. Your sincerely / Yours faithfully 您真诚/忠诚的（礼貌性用语）
Smith　　　　　　　　史密斯（姓名）
Marketing Manager　　销售经理（职位）
Shanghai Qianjin International Freight Forwarding Company
　　　　　　　上海前进国际货代公司（公司名称）

（一）Read and Translate 读语句，翻译句子内容

（1）We thank you for choosing our company.

中文：_____

（2）Thank you for choosing our company.

中文：_____

（3）I took the liberty of writing to you about our company.

中文：_____

（4）Please believe that we will provide the most professional freight forwarding services.

中文：_____

（5）Please feel free to contact us directly.

中文：_____

（6）We hope to receive your detailed inquiry soon.

中文：_____

（7）We are looking forward to having the chance of cooperating with you in the near future.

中文：_____

（8）I sincerely hope that we could establish a long-term cooperative relationship! Thanks again for your interest.

中文：_____

（二）Choose and Write 选择合适的单词，根据句意填写到电子邮件中

choose	choosing	State-Owned	State-Own	believe	believed
assured	assure	professional	profession	sincerely	sincere
cooperative		cooperate	Marketing Manager		Marketing
established		establish			

Dear Mr. Smith,

Thank you for_____（选择）our company. Our company was_____（建立）in 1993.We are a_____（集装箱）Freight Forwarding Company and also a _____（国有）Enterprise.

...

...

...

Please_____（相信） that we will provide the most_____（专业的）freight forwarding services. I_____（真诚地） hope that we could establish a long-term_____（合作） relationship! Thanks again for your interest.

Yours sincerely,

Chen Fei

_____（销售经理）

Shanghai Qianjin International Freight Forwarding Company

五、运用常见沟通方式的表达句型

先进入知识学苑（1-1-5）开展任务实施前的准备，学习表达建立合作关系的语句。

知识学苑（1-1-5）——表达建立合作关系的语句

1. We hope to establish a long-term business relationship with you.
我们希望与你们建立业务关系。
2. If you have any questions, please feel free to contact me at any time.
如果你有任何问题，请随时与我们联系。
3. I'm looking forward to our next meeting.
我期待着我们下次的见面。
4. I'd like to hear your suggestion.
我想听听您的建议。
5. We will fax the detailed information to you later.
我们后续将会把详细的资料传真给您。

Judge and Write 判断语句，改写语句，研习沟通技巧

小陈学习了常见沟通方式的表达句型，脚本中英文互译后，接下来进入培训的第五个环节的考察，小陈面临的挑战是根据情境撰写规范、礼貌的用语。

情境一：前进货运代理公司的业务部员工小陈接到领导通知，杭州娃哈哈有限公司最近正在寻找一家专业的货代公司作为合作伙伴，承揽公司所有的进出口业务，现要求小陈联系娃哈哈有限公司出口部经理王先生，向他详细介绍本货代公司的专业性和服务高效性，以此达成长期合作关系，请阅读下面对话，用横线画出不恰当的语句，在横线处填写完整对话。

Wang: Hello! I'm Wang Kun, an export manager of Wahaha. What can I do for you?

Chen: Hello! Mr. Wang, I'm Chen Fei, the marketing manager of ABC Freight Forwarding Company. I heard that you are looking for a professional forwarder company. If you haven't made up your mind, just pick us!

Wang: Well, do you have any experience in container import and export business?

Chen: Sure.

…

Chen: If you have any questions, Please contact us during working time.

_____
_____
_____
_____
_____
_____

情境二：小陈是上海前进货代公司的业务部经理，他在网上看到马克（Mark）发布的一则消息，法国JD服装设计公司正在网上搜索专业的货代公司，希望能与有运输高端服装经验的货代公司合作，帮助其开展将高端旗袍出口到中国的相关业务。小陈看到后，以电子邮件的形式介绍本公司。让我们一起来帮助小陈完成这份邮件吧。

Dear＿＿＿＿＿＿＿＿＿，（亲爱的马克先生）

＿＿＿＿＿＿＿＿（很高兴为您介绍我们公司）. Our company was established in Hangzhou in 2001. We have 1,000 branches all over the whole world. We make sure that your silk will receive class-A service.

Covering in both sea and air freight, our company has expertise in warehousing, transportation…packaging service and so on.

＿＿＿＿＿＿＿＿＿＿＿＿＿＿＿＿＿＿＿＿＿＿＿＿＿＿＿＿＿＿＿＿＿＿＿＿＿＿

＿＿＿＿＿＿＿＿（我们希望与你们建立业务关系。如果你有任何问题，请随时与我们联系）

Yours sincerely,

Chen Fei

＿＿＿＿＿＿＿＿＿＿＿＿＿＿＿＿＿＿＿＿＿＿＿＿＿＿＿＿＿＿＿＿＿＿（销售经理）

＿＿＿＿＿＿＿＿＿＿＿＿＿＿＿＿＿＿＿＿＿＿＿＿＿＿＿＿＿＿＿＿＿＿Company

【知识检测】

"货代销售中常见的沟通方式"这一任务的评价采用自测形式，请学生在实施任务后对于应掌握的词汇或句型进行回顾，完成Self-check，对于已掌握的，在它前面的括号中打"√"，完成表1-1-1的填写。

表1-1-1　常见的沟通方式知识自测表

Self-check	
I learned:	
（　）Freight Forwarding Company	（　）Import/Export Manager
（　）Hello! Is this ABC Freight Forwarding Company?	
（　）This is what I should do! Goodbye!	
（　）Good morning, sir ! It is a pleasure to meet you!	
（　）Welcome to our company, Mark , nice to meet you!	
（　）Please don't hesitate to ask me if you have any questions.	
（　）Please believe that we will provide the most professional freight forwarding services.	
（　）We are looking forward to having the chance of cooperating with you in the near future.	
（　）If you have any questions, please feel free to contact me at any time.	
I can:	
（　）communicate with clients in three common ways.	

Task Two Introduction to Freight Forwarding Services
任务二　货代公司业务介绍

【任务导入】

上海前进国际货代公司的实习销售人员小陈，顺利通过了培训测试。公司业务总监小飞分配给小陈的第一个工作任务是向客户罗伯特先生介绍本公司目前的货代业务情况。小陈下定决心，一定要完成好这个任务，与罗伯特先生顺畅地沟通。

请与小陈一起完成货代公司业务介绍吧！

【任务实施】

一、明确货代公司业务词汇

请先进入知识学苑（1-1-6）开展任务实施前的学习，认识货代公司常用的业务词汇。

知识学苑（1-1-6）——货代公司的业务词汇
1. FCL And LCL——整箱和拼箱 2. Warehousing And Consolidation——仓储集运 3. Customs Clearance——清关 4. Quarantine——检疫 5. Space Booking——订舱 6. Customs Brokerage——报关 7. Purchasing Order Processing——订单处理 8. Shipment Tracking——货物跟踪 9. EDI——电子数据交换 10. Bonded Trucking——报税托运 11. Assembling/dis- assembling——货物集中/分拨 12. Cartage——搬运

（一）Think and Match 读词汇，匹配业务名称

在"知识学苑"中学习了常见货代公司业务后，小陈认识了货代的相关业务，他尝试将常见货代公司的英文全称或英文缩写与它的中文名称匹配起来。

如图1-1-2，请将货代公司的英文表述与中文表述进行正确连线。

模块一 销 售

"连连看"——货代公司业务介绍相关词汇

仓储集运	Space Booking
订单处理	FCL and LCL
订舱	Purchasing Order Processing
报税托运	Warehousing and Consolidation
整箱和拼箱	Shipment Tracking
货物跟踪	EDI
电子数据交换	Customs Brokerage
清关	Customs Clearance
检疫	Quarantine
报关	Bonded Trucking
货物集中/分拨	Cartage
搬运	Assembling/dis-Assembling

图 1-1-2　常见描述货代公司业务相关词汇

（二）Read and Judge 读短文，判断业务内容

在完成货代公司业务介绍前，小陈还要明确一个业务推广的内容。阅读以下短文，完成与报价要素相关的判断，在正确表述前的方框内打"√"。

1. Read

Before introducing the company's freight forwarding business, you need to introduce yourself, ask customers what services they need, and introduce the main situation of the company to the guests (including the establishment time and address of the company, the size of the company, its position in the logistics industry, etc.).

When introducing the company's freight forwarding business, it is best to follow these guidelines: First of all, you should thank the customer for their consulting. Secondly, fully understand the services that customers need. Thirdly, fully provide the advantages of the company's business services, such as cartage, shipment tracking, customs brokerage, inspection declaration, LCL / FCL, one-stop-shop and so on. Finally, express the desire to establish a cooperative relationship.

【参考译文】

在介绍公司货代业务前,你需要自我介绍,询问客户需要什么服务,向客人介绍公司的主要情况(包括公司成立的时间和地址、公司规模、在物流行业中的地位等)。

在介绍公司货代业务中,最好遵守以下准则:第一,你应该感谢客户的咨询。第二,充分了解客户所需要的服务。第三,充分提供本公司业务服务的优势,如装箱、货物跟踪、报关、报检、整箱/拼箱、一站式服务等。最后,表达希望建立合作关系的愿望。

2. Judge

☐ (1) Before introducing the company's freight forwarding business, you don't have to introduce yourself.

☐ (2) It's necessary to show the company's position in the logistics industry while introducing your side.

☐ (3) You should thank the customer for their consulting before introducing your company's business.

☐ (4) Customs brokerage is not a part of the logistics company's business.

☐ (5) Barcode scanning is one part of the logistics company's business.

二、熟悉货代公司业务的常见句型

请先进入知识学苑(1-1-7)开展任务实施前的准备,学习货代公司业务介绍的口语句型。

知识学苑(1-1-7)——货代公司业务介绍的常见句型

货代公司业务推广既要明确说明公司的业务优势,也要注意用好礼貌用语,关注客户的感受,常见句型如下。

(一)**Giving regards to the customer** 向客人问好
1. Welcome to our company, Andy, nice to meet you.
2. I will show my warmest welcome to…

(二)**Self-introduction of the salesman** 业务员自我介绍
1. My name is…Here is my card.
2. First let me introduce myself. I'm…

(三)**Asking for the requirements of the customer** 询问客人需要什么服务
1. What can I do for you?
2. May I know what product you are interested in?

(四)**Introducing the company's main condition to the customer** 向客人介绍公司的主要情况
1. We started our logistics business in 1998 and now we are one of the top…
2. We are one of the biggest…
3. Our intermodal service covers almost each country throughout the world.

模块一 销售

续表

知识学苑（1-1-7）——货代公司业务介绍的常见句型

4. Our company has 60 offices in 40 cities all over the China.

（五）**Introducing the company's main business to the customer** 向客人介绍公司的主要业务

1. Our business covers import and export container transportation and agency, door to door pickup and delivery, warehousing and consolidation.

2. We specialize in logistics and distribution solutions.

3. Our company in China covers not only the transportation services, but also customs brokerage services and space booking services.

4. Our service covers almost each country throughout the world.

5. Our services can help you to reduce logistics cost and improve efficiency.

（六）Negotiating and cooperating with the customer 与客人洽谈合作

1. If you have any concerns, please let me know. I'm at your service 24hrs.

2. I'm sure you won't regret to choose us.

3. It is my pleasure.

（七）Wishing the pleasant cooperation 祝愿合作愉快

1. I believe we will have a good cooperation.

2. Wish a pleasant cooperation with you!

3. Wish we cooperate the delectation.

（一）Act and Read 扮角色，口语朗读

看到小陈愁眉不展的样子，业务总监小飞让经验丰富的小王和小陈做了角色扮演，通过角色扮演小飞能快速学会业务推广时的口语用语。

情境内容：小王扮演客户，现有一批家电需要急需从中国运往温哥华，故前来咨询。小陈针对小王的需求并结合公司现有优势进行了一个电话交谈：

Chen: Hello! This is QIANJIN freight forwarding company, can I help you?

Fei: Hello! May I speak to the export manager?

Chen: Speaking. Who's that, may I ask?

Fei: This is Andy from Wal-Mart Sales calling from Vancouver. We have learned that you are one of the members of FIATA.

Chen: That's right. What can I do for you?

Fei: We plan to import a bunch of appliances from China. I think it is our mutual advantage to establish business relationship.

Chen: Yes. I am sure you won't be disappointed to establish a business relationship with us.

Fei: Oh, actually we urgently need these goods, could you arrange delivery to Vancouver first?

Chen: OK, I get it .We have an effective transportation system. If we can sign the contract now, we will arrange delivery for you as soon as possible. It will take two days to arrive Vancouver.

Fei: Great. I will fax the detailed requirements to you later.

Chen: OK! Glad to be of service. Thank you for calling.

（二）Sort，Copy and Translate 排序、抄写和翻译对话

1. Sort 对话排序

小陈通过口语练习有了一定的基础，接下来做一个小测验。请对下面客户与业务员面对面交谈的对话做一个排序，用"a.b.c.d…"表示。

( ) Me too.

( ) Welcome to our company, Andy. Nice to meet you!

( ) We starting our logistics business in 2000, and now we are one of the Top 20 international freight and forwarders in the south of China.

( ) Andy, my name is Liu Jiang. Here is my card. I'm willing to introduce our company.

( ) OK.

( ) Thanks a lot.

( ) Uh-huh.

( ) We can provide integrated logistics services. Our business covers Air，Sea and land transportation.

( ) OK, I see. Do you have your own warehouse?

( ) Of course, we have more than 90,000 ㎡ warehouse spaces.

( ) If you have any concerns, please let me know. I'm at your service 24hrs.

( ) Well, you are welcome. I'd like to hear your suggestion.

( ) Can't wait to meet you.

( ) I hope so.

2. Copy and Translate 抄写，翻译业务面谈对话

小陈完成了与客户面谈对话的排序，经验丰富的小王看了后很满意。勤奋的小陈将对话以正确的顺序抄写了下来，再将上述对话翻译成了中文。

（a）英文：_____

中文：_____

（b）英文：_____

中文：_____

(c) 英文：_____
中文：_____
(d) 英文：_____
中文：_____
(e) 英文：_____
中文：_____
(f) 英文：_____
中文：_____
(g) 英文：_____
中文：_____
(h) 英文：_____
中文：_____
(i) 英文：_____
中文：_____
(j) 英文：_____
中文：_____
(k) 英文：_____
中文：_____

（三）Act and Practise 角色扮演，完成面谈任务

在通过以上口语、排序、翻译练习后，小陈打算和小王交换角色，以客户的身份来换位思考和提升业务能力。模拟情境为小王陈述近期的一次与客户交谈内容。主要是客户有一批瓷器需要运输和储存，正在寻找合适的物流公司，如果该公司有瓷器相关产品的服务经验且价格较低、运输速度快，你就会考虑与该公司长期合作。（同学两人一组，角色扮演，写好对话并进行口语交流。）

_____
_____
_____
_____
_____
_____
_____
_____

三、撰写货代公司业务服务的电子邮件

请先进入知识学苑（1-1-8）开展任务实施前的准备，学习用电子邮件形式来撰写货代业务。

知识学苑（1-1-8）——用电子邮件形式来撰写货代业务

Dear Mr./Mrs.××××，（称呼）

Thank you for×××××××××××××××（礼貌性地表示感谢的语句），Our company×××××××（公司的成立时间和地址，公司规模、员工人数、在物流行业中的地位等反映公司规模与地位的内容填写，吸引客户的关注。）

The major services we provide are listed as follow：××××××××××××××××（公司提供的主要业务服务有……，明确本公司的业务服务类型和能力，也可以提出更有特色的增值服务或者成功项目的举例等，让客户相信我们的能力并提高合作信心。）

We hope to××××××××××××/I sincerely hope that ××××××××××××××（表达合作愿景的语句。）

Yours sincerely,

×××××××（注明姓名）

Marketing Manager（注明职位）

×××××××（注明公司名称）

（一）Read 朗读邮件，提升实践技能

在"知识学苑"中学习了邮件表达的格式后，接下来朗读下面的一则邮件，提升业务表达能力。

邮件情境摘要：上海前进货代公司的业务部经理陈飞接到顾客 Celina 的咨询邮件。外商 Celina 长期从中国进口丝绸品，在网上看到前进货代公司广告，希望进一步了解该公司，如有可能将长期合作。陈飞需要写一封英文电子邮件，推广公司的货代业务。

Dear Celina,

Thank you for choosing our logistics company. Our company was established in Shanghai in 1998. We have 1,020 branches all over the whole world. We assure you of our best service. Our company is active in both sea and air freight, and has expertise in warehousing, transportation, distribution, express services, door to door service, packaging service and so on.

I sincerely hope that we could establish a long-term cooperative relationship! Thanks again for your interest.

Yours sincerely,

Chen Fei

Marketing Manager

Shanghai Qianjin Freight Forwarding Company

（二）Think and Practise 思考并判断，提升邮件语句的实践表达能力

在学习了撰写邮件格式和内容表达后，小陈尝试将邮件中表达的语句做一个判断，对下面语句表达正确的填（A），不恰当的填（B），并用横线划出不恰当的语句，在下方小框里填写正确的语句。

（　） ① Thank you for choosing our logistics company.

（　） ② I'm not surprised you chose our company.

（　） ③ Our company has just set up , and we have no experience in transportation.

（　） ④ Our company was established in Shanghai in 1998.We has a wealth of experience in transportation.

（　） ⑤ The major services we provide are listed as follows: warehousing, transportation, express services and so on.

（　） ⑥ At present, we only provide the transportation service.

（　） ⑦ We hope to receive your detailed inquiry soon.

（　） ⑧ I sincerely hope that we could establish a long-term relationship!

（三）Write and Talk 撰写货代公司业务的电子邮件

1. Write and Practice 撰写电子邮件，提升实践技能

在"知识学苑"中学习了电子邮件中语言的表达与业务介绍的格式，接下来小陈将

给客户罗伯特先生发一封电子邮件来介绍自己的公司。

公司概况：上海前进国际货代公司成立于 2000 年，是一家集装箱货运代理公司，如今已经成为领先的物流综合服务提供商，公司在国内拥有 500 家分公司。

公司提供的主要服务有：海洋货运、航空货运、仓储、配送。其他服务有报关、报检、货物跟踪和门到门服务等，最大的优点是能全方位为客户设计成本低、效率高的物流方案。（可适当扩展描述）

Dear＿＿＿＿＿＿＿＿＿＿，

2. Knowledge Development 知识拓展

小陈在发送好邮件后，又利用空余时间撰写了与客户面对面和电话交流的脚本，以此提升自己的业务表达能力。（同学两人一组，撰写脚本，角色扮演练习口语，提升技能。）

【知识检测】

"货代公司业务"这一任务的评价采用自测形式，请学生在实施任务后对于应掌握的词汇或句型进行回顾，完成 Self-check，对于已掌握的，在它前面的括号中打"√"，完成表 1-1-2 的填写。

模块一 销 售

表 1-1-2 货代公司业务知识自测表

Self-check
I learned:
（　）Warehousing and Consolidation　　　　（　）Space Booking
（　）Customs Brokerage　　　　　　　　　　（　）Bonded Trucking
（　）Customs Clearance　　　　　　　　　　（　）Quarantine
（　）We starting our logistics business in 1998 and now we are one of the top…
（　）Our business covers import and export container transportation and agency, door to door pickup and delivery, warehousing and consolidation.
（　）Our services can help you to reduce logistics cost, and improve the efficiency.
（　）Our intermodal service covers almost each country throughout the world.
（　）If you have any concerns, please let me know. I'm at your service 24hrs.
（　）I'm sure you won't be regret to establish business relationship with us.
（　）I believe we will have a good cooperation.
I can:
（　）introduce freight forwarding services in three common ways.

项目二
货代合同
Project Two Shipping Agency Agreement

【学习目标】

1. 掌握货代合同的基本英语词汇、句式和表达方式。
2. 能阅读进出口货代合同,并能根据自身需求调整、撰写部分条款。
3. 在学习货代合同的过程中,培养严谨求实的职业习惯。

Task One Export Shipping Agency Agreement
任务一 认识出口货代合同

【任务导入】

小王是上海前进国际货代公司出口部的实习操作员,他接到客户陈先生的来电,委托代理一批从上海港出口的女装,希望前进国际货代公司可以先拟定好出口货代合同初稿再进行磋商。

请与小王一起完成出口货代合同的拟定吧!

【任务实施】

一、明确出口货代合同的基本结构

请先进入知识学苑(1-2-1)开展任务实施前的学习,了解出口货代合同的基本结构。

知识学苑（1-2-1）——出口货代合同的基本结构

出口货代合同一般包括标题、签约日期和地点、签约方、鉴于条款、本文、签名这六个部分。

1. 标题（Heading）

EXPORT SHIPPING AGENCY AGREEMENT 出口货运代理合同

2. 签约日期和地点（Date and place）

Signed in（...place...）on（...date...）

通常为签订合同的日期和地点，也是合同生效的时间和地点。

3. 签约方（Parties）

Party A 甲方

Consigner 委托方（在出口货代合同中相当于甲方）

Party B 乙方

Consignee 受委托方（在出口货代合同中相当于乙方）

4. 鉴于条款（Whereas clause）

此条款通常说明签订合同的目的。

例：For the purpose of dealing with Sea freight shipments, through friendly consultations it has been agreed by the parties as follows.

就甲方委托乙方代办海运事宜，经双方友好协商，达成以下协议。

5. 本文（Body of the contract）

详细列明甲乙双方约定的责任义务、价款付款方式、违约责任等条款。

例：Party B is responsible for chartering, booking, customs declaration, inspection, signing and other related export business.

乙方负责为甲方办理出口的租船、订舱、报关、报检、签单等相关出口业务。

6. 签名（Seal）

通常甲乙双方在合同最后签字并盖章，合同生效。

（一）Think and Match 连一连，匹配合同各部分

在"知识学苑"中学习了出口货代合同的基本结构以后，小王尝试将合同各部分的内容与合同结构进行匹配。

如图1-2-1，请将合同各部分内容与合同结构进行正确连线：

项目二　货代合同

图1-2-1　出口货代合同结构配对

二、学习出口货代合同中的常用词汇

请先进入知识学苑（1-2-2）开展任务实施前的准备，学习订立出口货代合同的常用词汇：

知识学苑（1-2-2）——出口货代合同的常用词汇
for the purpose of … 为了……；目的是 deal with … 涉及……；处理…… clarify … 阐明；讲清…… standardize … 立下标准；规范…… through friendly consultations 经双方友好协商 it has been agreed by … as follows: 达成以下协议 Party A shall notify Party B … 甲方应告知乙方…… via 通过，借助于 Party B is responsible for … 乙方负责…… Keep … updated of the information of … 及时提供……的最新信息 Keep all information strictly confidential 对……信息严格保密 Include but not limit 包括但不限于 The currency of payment from Party A to Party B shall be … 甲方向乙方支付费用币种为…… Unless specified 除另有指明 Payment shall be made via … 支付方式是…… Commission … to handle insurance issues 委托……办理保险事宜

25

续表

知识学苑（1-2-2）——出口货代合同的常用词汇
Insurance premiums shall be borne by … 保险费由……承担 In case 假使，如果 non-B causes 非乙方原因 Herein 在此，在……过程中 Diligent Efforts 十分努力，尽心尽责 Be solved by … 以……的方式解决 Friendly negotiation 友好协商 Subject to … 服从……；受制于…… In duplicate 一式两份 Parties hereto 本合同双方 Remain in force 在有效期中，仍然有效 Settle all the costs 结清所有费用

Read and Match 读单词，匹配含义

在"知识学苑"中学习了出口货代合同常用词汇和句型后，小王尝试将每项词组的英文与它的中文含义匹配起来，如图 1-2-2 所示。

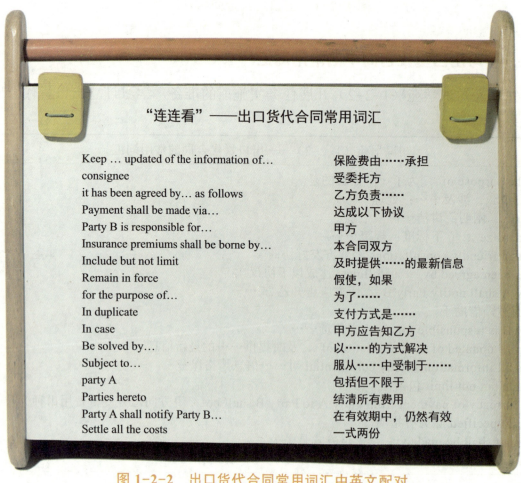

图 1-2-2　出口货代合同常用词汇中英文配对

三、草拟进口货代合同

请先进入知识学苑（1-2-3）开展任务实施前的准备，学习订立出口货代合同的常用条款表达：

知识学苑（1-2-3）——出口货代合同的常用表达

出口货代合同的主体部分主要规定了签约双方的出口货运代理事宜，以及在出口货代业务流程中双方的责任和义务、代理费用约定、保险、索赔及争议解决条款等。

出口货代合同常用的词汇和句型如下：

（一）鉴于条款有目的

1. For the purpose of dealing with Sea freight shipments, clarifying agency relations of both parties and standardizing operational specifications, through friendly consultations it has been agreed by the parties as follows:

（译文：为明确甲乙双方的代理关系，规范业务操作，经双方友好协商，就甲方委托乙方代办海运事宜，达成以下协议：）

（二）双方责任要细致

1. Party A shall notify Party B complete and authentic booking information before shipment of goods via Shipping Order.

（译文：甲方在货物出运前填制内容完整、真实的订舱单，通知乙方有关的货物出运信息。）

2. Party B is responsible for chartering, booking, customs declaration, inspection, signing and other related export business per requirements on Shipping Order confirmed by both parties.

（译文：乙方负责为甲方办理出口的租船、订舱、报关、报检、签单等相关出口业务，具体内容以甲方下达的订舱单为准。）

3. Party B shall notify and keep Party A updated of the information of shipment schedule timely for Party A's advanced plan and arrangement.

（译文：乙方应及时向甲方提供船期预报以及截止接单日期，作为甲乙双方办理海运订舱事宜的参考。）

4. Party B shall keep all information including but not limit customer data and related costs provided by Party A strictly confidential.

（译文：乙方保证对甲方提供的信息包括但不限于客户资料和相关费用严格保密。）

（三）代理费用要精确

1. The currency of payment from Party A to Party B shall be in RMB or USD unless specified.

（译文：甲方向乙方支付相关港口及海运费，除特别注明外，币种为人民币或者美元。）

2. Payment shall be made via telegraphic transfer to following account.

（译文：通过电汇的方式支付到以下乙方银行账号。）

3. 账号有关词汇：

Beneficiary Bank Name——开户银行

Address of Bank——开户银行地址

SWIFT CODE——SWIFT 代码

Account Name——银行户名

RMB Account No.——人民币账号

USD Account No.——美元账号

续表

知识学苑（1-2-3）——出口货代合同的常用表达
（四）保险条款要明晰 1. Party A may self-insure their consignment, and can also commission Party B to handle insurance issues. （译文：甲方可以对其托运的货物自行投保，也可委托乙方代为办理保险事宜。） 2. Insurance premiums shall be borne by Party A, the costs of which are not included in the those the two sides agreed. （译文：保险费由甲方承担，此费用不在双方约定的费用以内。） 3. In case Party A is not insured, Party B shall not be responsible for the damage from non-B causes. （译文：如甲方未予保险，则非乙方原因产生的货损乙方不予负责。） （五）索赔条款要明责 Party B must use Diligent Efforts to conduct and perform certain works herein for the delivery of Party A's goods. （译文：乙方在办理甲方货物出口运输的过程中应尽心尽责。） （六）争议条款论解决 1. Any dispute arising under this Contract shall be solved by friendly negotiation. （译文：本协议项下产生的任何争议，双方应友好协商。） 2. In case negotiation fails, it subjects to legal channels. （译文：协商不成，须通过法律途径解决。） (七）其他条款作补充 1. The contract is in duplicate, with each party holds one. （译文：本合同一式二份，双方各执一份。） 2. Parties hereto may revise or supplement through negotiation matters not mentioned herein. （译文：协议未尽事宜，甲乙双方另行商议，作为对协议的补充。） 3. The contract becomes effective since the date of signing and remains in force for one year. In case of renewal, another contract shall be needed. （译文：合同自签订之日起生效，有效期为一年，合同期限届满后如续约，则需另签。） 4. If either party terminates the contract in advance, it shall inform the other party in advance for one month and settle all the costs at one time. （译文：如一方提前解除合同，需提前一个月通知对方并一次性结清费用及退单。）

（一）Read and Translate 读合同，翻译合同条款

EXPORT SHIPPING AGREEMENT	
For the purpose of dealing with Sea freight shipments, clarifying agency relations of both parties and standardizing operational specifications, through friendly consultations it has been agreed by the parties as follows:	请翻译：

EXPORT SHIPPING AGENCY AGREEMENT	
Part one: Responsibilities and Obligations:	第一部分：甲乙双方责任、义务
Party A shall notify Party B complete and authentic booking information before shipment of goods via Shipping Order; Party B is responsible for chartering, booking, customs declaration, inspection, signing and other related export business per requirements on Shipping Order confirmed by both parties.	请翻译： 1.1
Party A is responsible for providing Party B authentic and consistent documents needed to conduct and perform duties and works (including packing lists, invoices, contracts, verification forms, customs proxy, Entrust Letter of Inspection, etc.).	1.2
Party B shall notify and keep Party A updated of the information of shipment schedule timely for Party A's advanced plan and arrangement.	1.3
...	...
Party B shall keep all information including but not limit customer data and related costs provided by Party A strictly confidential.	1.7
...	...

续表

EXPORT SHIPPING AGENCY AGREEMENT	
Part two: Accounting	第二部分：代理费用
...	...
The currency of payment from Party A to Party B shall be in RMB or USD unless specified. Payment shall be made via telegraphic transfer to following account. 　　Beneficiary Bank Name: 　　Address of Bank: 　　SWIFT CODE: 　　Account Name: 　　RMB Account No.: 　　USD Account No.:	2.2
...	...
Part three: Insurance	第三部分：保险条款
Party A may self-insure their consignment, and can also commission Party B to handle insurance issues, insurance premiums shall be borne by Party A, the costs of which are not included in the those the two sides agreed; In case Party A is not insured, Party B shall not be responsible for the damage from non-B causes.	请翻译：3.1
Part four: Claim Terms	第四部分：索赔条款
Party B must use Diligent Efforts to conduct and perform certain works herein for the delivery of Party A's goods. Party B shall be liable for all cost and damage caused to Party A due to failure of Party B, including but not limited the lost because of late delivery.	请翻译：4.1

续表

EXPORT SHIPPING AGENCY AGREEMENT	
...	...
Part five: Dispute Settlement	第五部分：争议解决条款
Any dispute arising under this Contract shall be solved by friendly negotiation. In case negotiation fails, it subjects to legal channels.	请翻译：
...	...
Part six: Miscellaneous	第六部分：其他
...	...
The contract is in duplicate, with each party holds one. Parties hereto may revise or supplement through negotiation matters not mentioned herein. The contract becomes effective since the date of signing and remains in force for one year. In case of renewal, another contract shall be needed. If either party terminates the contract in advance, it shall inform the other party in advance for one month and settle all the costs at one time.	6.6

（二）Remember and Complete 忆句型，补全出口货代合同

为了巩固学习成果，小王反复研究这份出口货代合同，努力记忆常用的词汇和句型，并在以下横线上填写缺失的部分词汇。

EXPORT SHIPPING AGENCY AGREEMENT
For the ___(1)___ of dealing with Sea freight shipments, clarifying agency relations of both parties and standardizing operational specifications, through friendly consultations it has been ___(2)___ by the parties as follows:
Part one: Responsibilities and Obligations:
Party A shall ___(3)___ Party B complete and authentic booking information before shipment of goods via Shipping Order; Party B is ___(4)___ for chartering, booking, customs declaration, inspection, signing and other related export business per requirements on Shipping Order confirmed by both parties.

EXPORT SHIPPING AGENCY AGREEMENT

Party A is responsible for __(5)__ Party B authentic and consistent documents needed to conduct and perform duties and works (including packing lists, invoices, contracts, verification forms, customs proxy, Entrust Letter of Inspection, etc.).

Party B shall __(6)__ and keep Party A __(7)__ of the information of shipment schedule timely for Party A's advanced plan and arrangement.

...

Party B shall keep all information including __(8)__ customer data and related costs provided by Party A strictly confidential.

...

Part two: Accounting

...

The currency of payment from Party A to Party B shall be in RMB or USD unless __(9)__. Payment shall be __(10)__ via telegraphic transfer to following account.

__(11)__ Bank Name:
Address of Bank:
SWIFT CODE:
Account Name:
RMB Account No.:
USD Account No.:

...

Part three: Insurance

Party A may __(12)__ their consignment, and can also commission Party B to handle insurance issues, insurance premiums shall be __(13)__ by Party A, the costs of which are not included in the those the two sides agreed; In __(14)__ Party A is not insured, Party B shall not be responsible for the damage from non-B causes.

Part four: Claim Terms

Party B must use Diligent __(15)__ to conduct and perform certain works herein for the delivery of Party A's goods. Party B shall be liable for all cost and damage caused to Party A due to failure of Party B, including but not limited the lost because of late delivery.

...

Part five: Dispute Settlement

Any __(16)__ arising under this Contract shall be solved by friendly __(17)__. In case negotiation fails, it __(18)__ to legal channels.

...

续表

EXPORT SHIPPING AGENCY AGREEMENT
Part six: Miscellaneous
...
The contract is in ___(19)___, with each party holds one. Parties ___(20)___ may revise or supplement through negotiation matters not mentioned herein. The contract becomes effective since the date of signing and remains in ___(21)___ for one year. In case of renewal, another contract shall be needed. If either party terminates the contract in advance, it shall inform the other party in advance for one month and ___(22)___ all the costs at one time.

（三）草拟出口货代合同

在前期的沟通中，小王对出口商的商品和需求已经有了了解，在反复梳理出口货代业务流程后，小王参照已有的出口货代合同，拟定了如下合同初稿。请将以下中文合同条款用英文表达出来，完成合同草拟。

1. 拟订标题

_____

（出口海运运输代理合同）

2. 签约时间

_____

（2020年8月1日）

3. 确定合同双方

_____

_____

（甲方：上海正兴服装有限公司　　乙方：上海前进国际货代公司）

4. 鉴于条款

_____

_____

_____

（为明确甲乙双方的代理关系，规范业务操作，经双方友好协商，就甲方委托乙方代办海运事宜，达成以下协议。）

5. 合同本文

第一部分：甲乙双方责任、义务

1.1_____

_____

（甲方在货物出运前填制内容完整、真实的订舱单，通知乙方有关的货物出运信息，乙方负责为甲方办理出口的租船、订舱、报关、报检、签单等相关出口业务，具体内容以甲方下达的订舱单为准。）

1.2_____

_____

[甲方负责为乙方提供办理业务所需要的单据（包括装箱单、发票、合同、核销单、报关委托书、报检委托书、合同、商检证书、许可证、报关单、手册及有关批文等），并对其内容的真实性和一致性负责。]

1.3_____

_____

（乙方应及时向甲方提供船期预报以及截止接单日期，作为甲乙双方办理海运订舱事宜的参考。）

1.4_____

_____

（请自行按需拟定适宜条款）

第二部分：代理费用

2.1_____

_____

（甲方向乙方支付相关港口及海运费，币种为人民币或者美元，乙方银行信息如下。）

2.2_____

_____

（请自行按需拟定适宜条款）

第三部分：保险条款

3.1_____

_____

（甲方可以对其托运的货物自行投保，也可以委托乙方代为办理保险事宜，保险费由甲方承担，此费用不在双方约定的费用以内，如甲方未予保险，则非乙方原因产生的货损乙方不予负责。)

3.2_____
_____
_____

(请自行按需拟定适宜条款)

第四部分：索赔条款

4.1_____
_____
_____

(在办理甲方货物出口运输的过程中应尽心尽责，对于因乙方的过失而导致甲方遭受的损失和发生的费用承担责任，以上损失包括但不限于货物因延迟等原因造成的经济损失。)

4.2_____
_____
_____

(请自行按需拟定适宜条款)

第五部分：争议解决条款

5.1_____
_____
_____

(本协议项下产生的任何争议，双方应友好协商。协商不成，须通过法律途径解决。)

5.2_____
_____
_____

(请自行按需拟定适宜条款)

第六部分：其他

6.1_____
_____
_____

(本合同一式两份，双方各执一份。协议未尽事宜，甲乙双方另行商议，作为对协议的补充。合同自签订之日起生效，有效期为一年，合同期限届满后如续约，则需另签。如一方提前解除合同，需提前一个月通知对方并一次性结清费用及退单。)

6.2_____

_____

_____

（请自行按需拟定适宜条款）

6.3 签名：

_____

_____

（甲乙双方签字盖章）

【知识检测】

"认识出口货代合同"这一任务的评价采用自测形式，请学生在实施任务后对于应掌握的词汇或句型进行回顾，完成 Self-check，对于已掌握的，在它前面的括号中打"√"，完成表 1-2-1 的填写。

表 1-2-1　认识出口货代合同知识自测表

Self-check		
I learned:		
（　）Heading	（　）Date and place	（　）Parties
（　）Party A	（　）Party B	（　）Consigner
（　）Consignee	（　）Seal	
（　）for the purpose of …		
（　）deal with …		
（　）clarify agency relations of both parties		
（　）standardize operational specifications		
（　）through friendly consultations		
（　）it has been agreed by … as follows		
（　）Party A shall notify Party B …		
（　）Party B is responsible for …		
（　）Keep … updated of the information of …		
（　）Include but not limit		
（　）The currency of payment from Party A to Party B shall be …		
（　）Unless specified		

续表

Self-check
( ) Payment shall be made via …
( ) Commission … to handle insurance issues
( ) Insurance premiums shall be borne by …
( ) In case …
( ) Be solved by …
( ) Subject to …
( ) In duplicate
( ) Parties hereto
( ) Remain in force
( ) Settle all the costs
I can:
( ) read and draft an export shipping agency agreement.

Task Two Import Shipping Agency Agreement
任务二　认识进口货代合同

【任务导入】

小李是上海前进国际货代公司进口部的实习操作员，他接到客户牛先生来电，准备委托前进国际货代公司代理一批从日本横滨港进口的冷藏三文鱼片。作为新手，小李有些紧张和不安，他担心无法拟订出让代理双方都满意的进口货代合同。

请与小李一起完成进口货代合同的起草吧！

【任务实施】

一、明确进口货代业务

请先进入知识学苑（1-2-4）开展任务实施前的学习，明确常见的进口货代业务。

知识学苑（1-2-4）——常见的进口货代业务

进口货代合同按照进口货代流程进行流转，进口货代流程规定了进口货代合同的主要履约内容。

（一）进口前准备阶段（Preparation before import）
（1）进口许可证申领——application for import license
（2）进口进货计划制订——make import plan

（二）签约阶段（Sign the contract）
（1）签订进口合同（FOB）——sign import contract（FOB）
（2）委托货代操作——entrust the forwarder

（三）履约阶段（Perform the contract）
1. 票据流转（bill circulation）
（1）申开信用证（issue L/C）
（2）付款（payment）
（3）赎单（redemption）
2. 货物流转（transport of goods）
（1）订舱（booking）
（2）发装运通知（notice of shipment）
（3）进口报关（import customs clearance）
（4）进口商检（import commodity inspection）
（5）提取货物（receive the goods）

（一）Think and Match 读词汇，匹配阶段名称

在"知识学苑"中学习了常见的进口货代业务后，小李知道了各阶段进口货代业务涉及的内容，他尝试将每项常见进口货代业务的英文名称与阶段名称匹配起来。

请将常见进口货代业务英文表述前的大写字母与进口货代流程阶段进行正确匹配。

属于进口前准备阶段（Preparation before import）的有：	属于签约阶段（Sign the contract）的有：	属于履约阶段（Perform the contract）的有：

A. sign import contract（FOB）　　B. import customs clearance　　C. booking
D. notice of shipment　　　　　　　E. application for import license　F. make import plan
G. receive the goods　　　　　　　 H. entrust the forwarder

（二）Read and Judge 读短文，判断进口货代合同要素

在与进口公司签订货运代理合同之前，小李还需要明确进口货运代理合同主要包括

哪些基本要素。阅读以下文章，完成进口货运代理合同基本要素正确性的判断，在正确的表述前面打"√"并进行朗读，在错误的表述前面打"×"并订正该说法。

1. Read

Before signing the freight forwarding contract, remember between the principal and the agent is through the agency agreement to determine the rights and obligations of both parties. Finding out which shipping companies and agents are allowed to carry the imported goods and figuring the method of obtaining a bill of lading for customs clearance.

We'd better start by contacting the shipping company (or shipping agency) in advance. Shipping company should provide the information of time and place to the port and name of the transit voyage. We need to accurately grasp the time and cost of changing the order. Don't forget to contact the container terminal in advance to determine the cost.

Finally, the distribution of benefits and cost settlement (customs declaration and inspection etc.) between the parties should also be written in the contract.

【参考译文】

在与进口商订立代理合同之前，要明确委托方与代理方之间是通过代理合同来确定双方的权利和义务的。先与进口商明确其进口货物允许使用哪家船公司承运、哪家船代公司作为代理、在哪里获取进口所需的提货单。

在被委托方告知相关信息后可与船公司（船代公司）提前取得联系，船公司会提供船到岗时间、地点以及中转的相关信息，以便我们及时将换单的时间和费用在代理合同中明确。另外也要提前联系场站确认其他产生的费用。

最后，双方的利益分配以及其他费用结算（报关和报检等）同样也应该被订立在双方代理合同里。

2. Judge

☐ (1) Before signing the freight forwarding contract, we know the agency agreement to determine the obligations only.

☐ (2) We'd better start by contacting the general administration of customs in advance.

☐ (3) Shipping company should provide the information of time and place to the port and name of the transit voyage.

☐ (4) The distribution of benefits and cost settlement between the parties should be written in the contract.

二、熟悉进口货代合同常用句型

请先进入知识学苑（1-2-5）开展任务实施前的准备，学习订立进口货运代理合同的典型语句。

知识学苑（1-2-5）——进口货代合同的典型句型

进口货运代理合同既要对责任划分、时空场所、利润分配作出详尽规定，也要明晰进口商销售细节和双方收付款项的细节，关注进口商的感受，典型句型如下。

（一）权责主体要明确

1. This agreement is entered into by … and …
　（译文：合同由……和……订立）
2. The parties agree to cooperate with one another for the purpose of …
　（译文：双方订立合同是出于……的考量）
3. The parties agree to follow the instructions and procedures …
　（译文：各方达成对……过程或步骤的遵循）

（二）委托事宜应准确

1. … appoints … as its break bulk agent in China.
　（译文：……指定……为中国的分拨代理）
2. Each party shall render service in customs clearance and delivery.
　（译文：双方都应该为彼此提供清关和运送服务）
3. You should only be allowed to place booking with our respective carriers:
　（译文：贵方只能向以上船公司联系订舱服务，包括……）
4. Under no circumstance should your company be allowed to …
　（译文：任何情况下贵方不得……）

（三）利润分配需精确

1. The parties hereby agree to share profit on routed shipments on a … %/ … % basis.
　（译文：双方同意按照航程……分配利润）
2. Profit shall be based on the … and …
　（译文：利润分享基础是……和……）
3. … shall not be subjected to profit share.
　（译文：……不列入利益分配之内）

（四）信息沟通必正确

1. The parties agree to fully and accurately disclose …
　（译文：双方同意全面而真实的共享……的信息）
2. … will be exchanged regularly.
　（译文：……的信息应定期交换）

（五）清算货款保正确

1. The parties agree to be fully responsible for the collection of …
　（译文：双方各自承担收取……费用的责任）
2. The parties further agree to be responsible for all payments to…in their respective countries.
　（译文：双方在各自国家付清关于……等方面的费用）
3. Unless otherwise agreed to in writing, the parties agree to cover at their…
　（译文：除非有其他约定，否则双方各自承担自身……的费用）

（一）Match and Fill 做匹配，补全句子

1. Match

在"知识学苑"中学习了订立进口货运代理合同的典型句型后，小李熟悉了不少订立进口合同的词组，他尝试将每项词组的英文全称与它的中文名称匹配起来。

请在图 1-2-3 中进行正确连线。

图 1-2-3　进口货代合同常用词汇中英文配对

2. Fill

根据"知识学苑"学习的订立进口货运代理合同的典型句型，选用合适的"介词"补全下列句子：

（1）Each party shall render service＿＿＿＿customs clearance and delivery.

（2）The parties hereby agree to share profit＿＿＿＿routed shipments＿＿＿＿a 50%/50% basis.

（3）The parties agree to be fully responsible＿＿＿＿the collection of all air freight in their respective countries.

（4）Under no circumstance＿＿＿＿should Part B be allowed＿＿＿＿switch booking to any other carriers.

（5）The parties agree to cover＿＿＿＿their own cost all expenses.

（二）Read and Translate 读函电，翻译进口货代合同

资深进口销售员老陈翻箱倒柜，找出了一份不涉密的进口货代合同供要完成此项任务的小李学习，这是之前上海前进国际货代公司进口部为某企业 S 从美国进口货品前签订的代理合同。勤快的小李仔细翻看合同，将有用的关键信息都翻译了出来，并在自己的笔记本上加以提炼总结，以便缮制自己将要起草的进口合同。

IMPORT AIR FREIGHT AGENCY AGREEMENT	
The agreement, made and entered into on this 20th day of June, 2020 by and between S company (hereinafter known as Part A) and Shanghai Qianjin Freight Forwarding Company (hereinafter known as Part B).	请翻译：
Part one：Purpose and Responsibilities	第一部分：责任规定
The parties agree to cooperate with one another for the purpose of developing airfreight business. The parties further agree to follow the instructions and procedures.	请翻译：
Part two：Entrusted matters	第二部分：委托事宜
Part A appoints Part B as its break bulk agent in China. Each party shall render service in customs clearance and delivery. Part B should only be allowed to place booking with our respective carriers: China Shipping, COSCO, and APL. Under no circumstance should Part B be allowed to switch booking to any other carriers.	请翻译：
Part three：Profit Share	第三部分：利益分配
The parties hereby agree to share profit on routed shipments on a 50%/50% basis. Profit shall be based on the difference between the agent's buying and selling rate. Trucking charges shall not be subject to profit share.	请翻译：
Part four：Disclosure	第四部分：信息披露

续表

IMPORT AIR FREIGHT AGENCY AGREEMENT	
The parties agree to fully and accurately disclose all airline buying rates. The parties further agree to disclose all details of new business development.	请翻译：
Part five: Payment	第五部分：结算付款
The parties agree to be fully responsible for the collection of all air freight in their respective countries. The parties further agree to be responsible for all payments to airlines. Unless otherwise agreed to in writing, the parties agree to cover at their own cost all expenses.	请翻译：
...(IN CONSIDERATION AND ACCEPTANCE OF THE ABOVE CONDITIONS)	

（三）Remember and Complete 忆句型，补全进口货代合同

为了巩固学习成果，小李反复研究这份进口货代合同，努力记忆进口货代合同的句型搭配和常用句式，并在以下横线上填写缺失的部分词汇。

IMPORT AIR FREIGHT AGENCY AGREEMENT
The agreement, made and ___(1)___ into on this 20th day of June, 2020 by and between S company (hereinafter known as Part A) and Shanghai Qianjin Freight Forwarding Company (hereinafter known as Part B).
Part one: Purpose and Responsibilities
The parties ___(2)___ to cooperate with one another for the purpose of developing air freight business. The parties further ___(3)___ to ___(4)___ the instructions and procedures.
Part two: Entrusted matters
Part A ___(5)___ Part B ___(6)___ its break bulk agent in China. Each party shall render ___(7)___ in customs clearance and delivery. Part B should only be ___(8)___ to place booking with our respective carriers: China Shipping, COSCO, and APL. Under no ___(9)___ should Part B be allowed to switch booking to any other carriers.
Part three: Profit Share
The parties hereby agree to share ___(10)___ on routed shipments on a 50%/50% basis. Profit shall be ___(11)___ on the difference between the agent's buying and selling rate. Trucking charges shall not be ___(12)___ to profit share.

续表

IMPORT AIR FREIGHT AGENCY AGREEMENT
Part four: Disclosure
The parties ___(13)___ to fully and accurately disclose all airline buying rates. The parties further agree to ___(14)___ all details of new business development.
Part five: Payment
The parties agree to be fully ___(15)___ for the collection of all air freight in their respective countries. The parties further agree to be ___(16)___ for all payments to airlines. Unless ___(17)___ agreed to in writing, the parties agree to cover at their own cost all expenses.

三、草拟进口货代合同

请先进入知识学苑（1-2-6）开展任务实施前的准备，学习订立出口货代理合同的常用条款表达。

知识学苑（1-2-6）——进口货运代理合同框架
进口货运代理合同基本框架如下。 1. 拟订标题（Formulate the title） 2. 确定合同双方（Confirm the parties to the contract） 3. 明确合同内容（Determine the content of contract） 　（1）明确责任规定（Purpose and responsibilities）。 　（2）明确委托事宜（Entrusted matters）。 　（3）明确利益分配（Profit share）。 　（4）明确信息披露（Disclosure）。 　（5）明确结算付款（Payment）。 4. 订立合同（Conclusion of the contract） 　（1）确定落款（Make signature）。 　（2）双方签字盖章（Seal）。

在前期的沟通中，小李对进口商的商品和需求已经有了了解，在反复梳理出口货代业务流程后，小李参照已有的进口货代合同，拟订了如下合同初稿。请将以下中文合同条款用英文表达出来，完成合同草拟。

1. 拟订标题

_____

（进口海运运输代理合同）

2. 确定合同双方

_____

_____

（甲方：上海市闵行区江滨商行　乙方：上海前进国际货代公司）

3. 确定合同内容

_____

_____

（拟订：责任规定、委托事宜、利益分配、信息披露、结算付款共五部分具体内容）

4. 确定落款双方签字盖章

_____

_____

（双方考虑并接受上述条件）

5. 责任规定

(1) _____

_____

（双方同意就空运事宜展开合作）

(2) _____

_____

_____

（双方进一步达成一致：遵守指示和程序）

6. 委托事宜

(1) _____

_____

（甲方委托乙方在中国作为其分拨代理）

(2) _____

_____

（甲乙双方都应该为彼此提供清关和运输的方便）

(3) _____

_____

（乙方指定甲方选择船公司承运，包括：商船三井、中国远洋、长荣海运。在任何情况下甲方都不能更改承运的船公司）

7. 利益分配

(1) _____

（甲乙双方按照运输船次的 60% 和 40% 分享利益）

(2) _____

（操作费 SOC 不在利益分配的范围之内）

8. 信息披露

_____

（双方同意全面而真实地共享关于海运过程的所有信息）

9. 结算付款

(1) _____

（双方同意全权负责各自国家的所有海运费用的收取）

(2) _____

（双方协商一致给付船公司所有款项）

(3) _____

（除非另有书面约定，双方同意自费支付包括卫检费 HEC 在内的所有费用。）

【知识检测】

"认识进口货代合同"这一任务的评价采用自测形式，请学生在实施任务后对于应掌握的词汇或句型进行回顾，完成 Self-check，对于已掌握的，在它前面的括号中打"√"，完成表 1-2-2 的填写。

表 1-2-2　认识进口货代合同知识自测表

Self-check
I learned:
（　）Preparation before import　｜　（　）Sign the contract
（　）Perform the contract　｜　（　）Transport of goods
（　）be entered into by … and …
（　）be agree to …
（　）appoints … as …
（　）service in …
（　）be allowed to …
（　）Under no circumstance …
（　）share profit on …
（　）be subjected to …
（　）be responsible for …
（　）Unless otherwise agreed to …
I can:
（　）read and draft an import shipping agency agreement.

Module Two　Marine Freight Transport
模块二　海　运

项目一
海运报价
Project One　Sea Quotations

【学习目标】

1. 能沟通完成海运电话报价。
2. 能阅读客户的海运询价邮件，并撰写海运报价邮件。
3. 在学习海运报价的过程中，培养严谨求实的职业习惯。

Task One　Sea Telephone Quotation
任务一　海运电话报价

【任务导入】

小余是上海前进国际货代公司的实习销售人员，前期联系的客户中有一位与企业长期合作的老客户——杰克先生，准备打电话向小余进行海运运费的询价。

作为一名货代销售岗位的新人，小余心里十分忐忑，担心无法与杰克先生顺畅地沟通。

请与小余一起完成海运电话报价吧！

【任务实施】

一、明确海运报价要素

请先进入知识学苑（2-1-1）开展任务实施前的学习，认识常见的海运运费种类。

> 知识学苑（2-1-1）——常见的海运运费种类
>
> 海运报价中涵盖了海运基本运费和海运附加费，以下为部分重要海运运费种类。
>
> （一）海运基本运费
> 1. Basic Sea Freight——基本海运费
> 2. FAK=Freight for All Kinds——均一包箱费率
> 3. FCS=Freight for Class——按不同货物等级制定的包箱费率
> 4. FCB=Freight for Class or Basis——既按不同货物等级，又按计算标准制定的包箱费率
>
> （二）海运附加费
> 1. BAF=Bunker Adjustment Factor——燃油附加费
> 2. CAF=Currency Adjustment Factor——货币贬值附加费
> 3. CY Charge=Container Yard Charge——集装箱堆场费用
> 4. DDC=Destination Delivery Charge——目的港交货费
> 5. GRI=General Rate Increase——综合费率上涨附加费
> 6. PCS=Port Congestion Surcharge——港口拥挤附加费
> 7. PSS=Peak Season Surcharge——旺季附加费
> 8. booking charge——订舱费
> 9. customs clearance fee——报关费
> 10. drayage charge——拖柜费

（一）Think and Match 读词汇，匹配费用名称

在"知识学苑"中学习了常见海运运费种类后，小余认识了不少海运附加费，他尝试将每项常见海运附加费的英文全称或英文缩写与它的中文名称匹配起来。

如图 2-1-1 所示，请将海运附加费的英文表述与中文表述进行正确连线。

图 2-1-1　常见海运附加费中英文配对

模块二　海　运

（二）Read and judge 读短文，判断报价要素

在完成海运电话报价前，小余还要明确一个标准的货运报价（不仅仅是海运报价）究竟应该包含哪些要素。阅读以下短文，完成与报价要素相关的判断，在正确表述前的方框内打"√"。

1. Read

Before providing a quotation, you need to inquire the customer about the name of the commodity, the shipment and destination port, the mode of transport, the weight, dimension and volume of the commodity, and other requirements.

When giving a quotation, it is advisable to observe the following guidelines：First, thank the inquirer for his/her inquiry, mention the date of the inquiry. Second, give the information fully: freight rate, carrier, frequency, routing, transit time, validity period, other charges etc. Finally, express the hope of a lasting friendly business relationship.

【参考译文】

在货运报价前，你需要询问客户的货物名称、出发地和目的地、运输方式、路线、货物重量、尺寸、货量以及其他要求。

在报价中，最好遵守以下准则。首先，你应该感谢客户的询价，并提及询价日期。其次，充分提供以下信息：运费、承运人、运输频率、路线、运输时间、有效期、其他费用等。最后，表达建立长期友好业务关系的希望。

2. Judge

☐ (1) Before providing a quotation, you need to inquire the customer about a lot of items for his/her cargo.

☐ (2) When you give a quotation, you should first give the information.

☐ (3) Your quotation should include:freight rate, carrier, frequency, routing, transit time, validity period, other charges etc.

☐ (4) You needn't express the hope of a lasting friendly business relationship.

二、学习海运电话报价句型

请先进入知识学苑（2-1-2）开展任务实施前的准备，学习海运电话报价的典型语句。

知识学苑（2-1-2）——海运电话报价的典型句型
海运电话报价既要明确说明海运报价的数值，也要注意用好礼貌用语，关注客户的感受，典型句型如下。

续表

知识学苑（2-1-2）——海运电话报价的典型句型

（一）接通电话有"温度"
1. Hello, this is … calling/speaking. What can I do for you?
2. Thank you for calling …
3. May I speak with …, please?

（二）客户询价有"准度"
1. I would like to have … shipped from … to …
2. Can you make me a quotation for …?
3. Please let me know the frequency and the transit time.

（三）销售报价有"精度"
1. How many containers are used and what size?
2. Our sea freight rate is …, including …
3. The … charge is …

（四）沟通遇困有"稳度"
1. Hold on, please. Let me check.
2. Sorry to keep you waiting.
3. Could you please repeat that?
4. Could you speak a little slower please.

（五）电话尾声有"风度"
1. I've got it, thank you.
2. I'll call you when I've made my decision.
3. Let me repeat that just to make sure.
4. I'm looking forward to your early reply.

（一）Choose and Answer 做选择，回答下列问题

看到小余愁眉不展的样子，经验丰富的货代销售员老李让小余做了五道选择题，希望他能从中体会电话报价的句型与面对面沟通的语句有什么不同。

1. Choose

小余复习了模块一中学过的电话沟通的常用句型，从每一题的A、B两种表述中，选择适合在海运电话报价中采用的语句，在括号内打"√"。

1) （   ）A. Hello!
   （   ）B. How do you do!

2) （   ）A. I'd like to talk to Michael.
   （   ）B. Can I speak to Michael, please?

3) （   ）A. Are you Michael?
   （   ）B. Is that Michael?

模块二 海 运

4) (   ) A. This is Mr. Yu from Shanghai Qianjin International Forwarder Co., Ltd.

(   ) B. I am Mr. Yu from Shanghai Qianjin International Forwarder Co., Ltd.

5) (   ) A. Take it easy.

(   ) B. Hold on, please.

2. Answer

在通过以上五道选择题的考验后，小余尝试回答以下问题。

Question: What is the difference between telephone communication and face-to-face communication?

_____
_____
_____
_____

（二）Read and Translate 读对话，翻译电话报价

资深货代销售员老李对于小余的回答很满意，答应了小余提出的拜师学习的请求。勤快的小余跟随在老李左右，将老李的海运电话报价实录整理出来，并利用空余时间将英文翻译为中文。

Mr. Li: Hello! This is Shanghai Qianjin International Forwarder Co., Ltd. What can I do for you?

译文：_____

Michael: I would like to have some precision instruments shipped from Hangzhou, China to Yokohama, Japan. Can you make me a quotation for DOOR TO PORT shipment?

译文：_____

Mr. Li: Sure. How many containers are used and what size?

译文：_____

Michael: Two 20-foot containers.

译文：_____

Mr. Li: Hold on, please. Let me check. (After a while)

译文：_____

Mr. Li: Sorry to keep you waiting. Our sea freight rate is USD 800, including Bunker Adjustment Factor, and Currency Adjust Factor. The container yard charge is 1590 RMB. The booking charge is 240 RMB. The drayage charge from Hangzhou to Ningbo is 2100 RMB. Besides, Customs clearance charge is 180 RMB per shipment.

译文：_____

Michael: Please let me know the frequency and the transit time.
译文：_____

Mr. Li: Every Monday, and this sea transport would take 4 days.
译文：_____

Michael: I've got it. Thank you, and I'll call you when I've made my decision.
译文：_____

Mr. Li: I'm looking forward to your early reply.
译文：_____

（三）Remember and Complete 忆句型，补全电话报价

为了巩固学习成果，小余反复研究老李的电话报价实录，努力记忆海运电话报价的典型句型，并在以下横线上填写了缺失的部分词汇。

Mr. Li: Hello!_____ _____ Shanghai Qianjin International Forwarder Co.,Ltd. What_____ _____ _____ for you?　　（接通电话有"温度"）

Michael: I would like to _____ some precision instruments _____ _____ Hangzhou, China _____ Yokohama, Japan. Can you _____ me a _____ for DOOR TO PORT shipment?　　（客户询价有"准度"）

Mr. Li: _____. _____ _____ containers are used and what size?

Michael: Two 20-foot containers.

Mr. Li: _____ _____, please. Let me check. (After a while)
　　　　　　　　　　　　　　　　　　　　　　（沟通遇困有"稳度"）

Mr. Li: Sorry to _____ you waiting. Our _____ _____ rate is USD 800, _____ _____ Bunker Adjustment Factor, and Currency Adjust Factor. The container yard charge is 1,590 RMB. The booking _____ is 240 RMB. The drayage charge from Hangzhou to Ningbo is 2,100 RMB. Besides, _____ clearance charge is 180 RMB per shipment.　　（销售报价有"精度"）

Michael: Please _____ _____ _____ the frequency and the transit time.　　（客户询价有"准度"）

Mr. Li: Every Monday, and this sea transport _____ _____ 4 days.
　　　　　　　　　　　　　　　　　　　　　　（销售报价有"精度"）

Michael: I've _____ it. Thank you, and I'll call you when I've _____ _____decision.

　　Mr. Li: I'm_____ _____to your early reply. （电话尾声有"风度"）

三、实施海运电话报价任务

请先进入知识学苑（2-1-3）开展任务实施前的准备，学习我国参与国际海运涉及的主要航线和所能到达的主要港口。

知识学苑（2-1-3）——中国主要海运航线与到达港口	
（一）远洋航线	
涉及航线名称	到达的主要港口
1. 地中海线	贝鲁特、的黎波里、海法、阿什杜德、塞得港、亚历山大、突尼斯、阿尔及尔、热那亚、马赛、巴塞罗那、利马索尔
2. 西北欧线	安特卫普、鹿特丹、汉堡、不来梅、勒弗尔、伦敦、利物浦、哥本哈根、奥斯陆、斯德哥尔摩、哥德堡、赫尔辛基
3. 北美西海岸线	温哥华、西雅图、波特兰、旧金山、洛杉矶、蒙特利尔、多伦多
4. 北美东海岸线	纽约、波士顿、费城、巴尔的摩、新奥尔良、休斯敦
5. 南美洲西岸线	卡亚俄、阿里卡、安托法加斯塔、瓦尔帕莱索
（二）近洋航线	
涉及航线名称	到达的主要港口
1. 港澳线	中国香港、中国澳门
2. 新马线	新加坡、马来西亚的巴生港、槟城、马六甲
3. 暹罗湾线	泰国曼谷、越南海防、柬埔寨磅逊
4. 科伦坡、孟加拉湾线	科伦坡、仰光、吉大港、加尔各答
5. 菲律宾线	菲律宾的马尼拉港
6. 印度尼西亚线	爪哇岛的雅加达、三宝垄等港
7. 澳大利亚新西兰线	澳大利亚的悉尼、墨尔本、布里斯班，新西兰的奥克兰、惠灵顿
8. 巴布亚新几内亚线	巴布亚新几内亚的莱城、莫尔兹比港
9. 日本线	日本的门司、神户、大阪、名古屋、横滨、川崎等港
10. 韩国线	韩国的釜山、仁川等港
11. 波斯湾线	巴基斯坦的卡拉奇，伊朗的阿巴斯、霍拉姆沙赫尔，伊拉克的巴士拉，科威特的科威特港，沙特阿拉伯的达曼

（一）Write and Talk 写脚本，练习电话报价

从前期沟通中，小余对即将电话沟通的杰克先生的商品和需求已经有所了解。为了顺利沟通，他参照资深货代销售员老李的电话报价实录，为自己拟定了如下海运电话报

价的中文提纲，并据此写出英文对话。

1. Write

小余：我是上海前进国际货代公司的小余。请问我能为您做些什么？

Mr. Yu: _____

杰克：我想要把一批家具从大连托运到德国的汉堡港。能不能给我提供门到港的海运报价？

Jack: _____

_____

小余：当然可以。请问您将会用多少个集装箱，规格是多少？

Mr. Yu: _____

_____

杰克：8 个 40 英尺货柜。

Jack: _____

小余：稍等，让我查一查。（一会儿以后）抱歉，让您久等了。我们的海运费是 1 850 美元，其中包含了燃油附加费、综合费率上涨附加费和旺季附加费。此外，订舱费是人民币 300 元，清关费是人民币 200 元。此报价在 2019 年 12 月 20 日前有效。

Mr. Yu: _____

_____

_____

杰克：请告诉我运输的频率和航程需要的时间。

Jack: _____

小余：每周四开船，运输大约需要 36 天。

Mr. Yu: _____

杰克：我已经接收到这些信息了。等我决定了会再给你打电话的。

Jack: _____

小余：期待您与我们进一步合作。

Mr. Yu: _____

2. Talk

请与同桌练习这部分电话报价。

（二）Act and Practise 扮角色，实施电话报价

与同桌或前后座同学组成两人小组，分别扮演上海前进国际货代公司的销售员小余和他的客户杰克。

（1）"客户杰克"在国际货代、物流公司网站查询海运航线信息，搜索中国各港口

城市到近洋航线、远洋航线上不同港口的航线信息；设定托运客户询价的信息；设计海运电话询价的语句。具体见表 2-1-1。

表 2-1-1　海运电话询价信息设计表

货物名称	
启运地	
目的港	
所用集装箱规格	
所用集装箱数量	
海运电话询价语句摘要	

（2）"销售员小余"在国际货代、物流公司网站查询海运航线信息，搜索中国各港口城市到近洋航线、远洋航线上不同港口的航线信息；根据实际航线的海运费用设定国际货代企业报价的信息；设计海运电话报价的语句。具体见表 2-1-2。

表 2-1-2　海运电话报价信息设计表

海运费	
海运费项目	
运输时间	
运输频率	
承运人	
报价有效期	
海运电话报价语句摘要	

（3）"客户杰克"与"销售员小余"在电话报价信息设计表的辅助下，开展对话交流，进行海运电话报价。

（4）对话后，"客户杰克"与"销售员小余"分别用不同颜色的笔对电话报价信息设计表进行修改。

（5）交换角色，再次完成（1）～（4），充分实践海运电话报价。

【知识检测】

"海运电话报价"这一任务的评价采用自测形式，请学生在实施任务后对于应掌握的词汇或句型进行回顾，完成 Self-check，对于已掌握的，在它前面的括号中打"√"，完成表 2-1-3 的填写。

表 2-1-3　海运电话报价知识自测表

Self-check				
I learned:				
	（　）BAF	（　）CAF	（　）CY Charge	（　）customs clearance fee
	（　）DDC	（　）GRI	（　）drayage charge	（　）booking charge
	（　）PCS	（　）PSS		
（　）Hello, this is ... calling/speaking. What can I help you?				
（　）How many containers are used and what size?				
（　）Our sea freight rate is ..., including ...				
（　）The ... charge is ...				
（　）Please let me know the frequency and the transit time.				
（　）Hold on, please. Let me check.				
（　）I've got it. Thank you , and I'll call you when I've made my decision.				
（　）I'm looking forward to your early reply.				
I can:				
（　）make sea quotation by telephone.				

Task Two　Sea Email Quotation
任务二　海运邮件报价

【任务导入】

小余是上海前进国际货代公司的实习销售人员，新客户威廉先生向小余发来邮件进行海运运费的询价。小余还是第一次用邮件进行报价呢，他十分希望自己能顺利完成任务。

请与小余一起完成海运邮件报价吧！

【任务实施】

一、读懂海运询价邮件

请先进入知识学苑（2-1-4）开展任务实施前的学习，熟悉海运询价邮件的内容。

> 知识学苑（2-1-4）——海运询价邮件的内容
>
> 在实施海运邮件报价之前，先要能读懂客户发来的海运询价邮件。那么海运询价邮件应该包含哪些内容呢？
>
> Inquires in sea freight forwarding are requests for information on sea freight rates, shipping spaces, frequency and transit time etc. Also it is very much worth mentioning that in sea freight inquiries, it is advisable to specify the following items for your shipment, the name of the commodity, origin port and destination port, preferred mode of transport/carrier.

【参考译文】

对海运货代进行询价，就是要求你提供海运费率、舱位、运输频率、运输时间等信息。同样非常重要的是，在海运询价中，最好明确有关托运货物的下列详情：商品名称、装运港和目的港、首选运输方式或承运人。

（一）Think and Match 读词汇，匹配词汇名称

在"知识学苑"中学习了海运询价邮件的内容后，小余对于海运询价邮件中经常出现的词汇有了印象，他尝试将这些词汇的英文与它们的中文名称匹配起来，如图 2-1-2 所示。

图 2-1-2　海运询价邮件内容中英文配对

模块二 海 运

（二）Read and judge 读短文，判断询价要领

在明确海运询价邮件的主要内容后，小余对于海运询价的要领也进行了学习。阅读以下短文，完成与询价要领相关的判断，在正确表述前的方框内打"√"。

1. Read

When making an inquiry, it is advisable to observe the following guidelines.

First, you may begin with the sentence by introducing yourself/your company. If you and the person/company you send inquiries to know each other very well, you just need to state the subject of your inquiry.

Second, for each item of information you want, better to use a separate paragraph.

Third, keep your inquiry brief, specific and to the point; say what needs to be said, ask what needs to be asked and no more. Then close with a simple "thank you" or "awaiting your reply" "looking forward to your response" etc.

Fourth, avoid using long, big, stale words and those over-polite and very formal phrases.

【参考译文】

在进行询价时，建议遵循以下原则：

（1）你可以从介绍你自己或你的公司开始。如果你和你询问的人（公司）彼此非常了解，那么你只需声明你询价的主题即可。

（2）对于每一项你想要询价的信息，最好用一个单独的段落。

（3）让你的询价简洁、具体、切中要点；说该说的，问该问的，不要多说。然后以简单的"谢谢"或"等待您的回复""期待您的回复"等结尾。

（4）避免使用冗长、夸张、陈旧的词和那些过于礼貌和过于正式的短语。

2. Judge

☐ (1) When making an inquiry, you just need to state the subject of your inquiry.

☐ (2) For each item of information you want to inquire, better to use a separate paragraph.

☐ (3) When making an inquiry, keep your inquiry brief, specific and to the point. Then close with a simple "thank you" or "awaiting your reply" "looking forward to your response" etc.

☐ (4) To be more polite, you may use long, big words and those over-polite and very formal phrases when making an inquiry.

（三）Read and Translate 读邮件，翻译询价邮件

在学习了海运询价邮件的内容和要领后，小余仔细阅读了客户威廉发来的询价邮件，如图 2-1-3 所示，尝试着将英文邮件翻译为中文，并回答问题。

1. Read

From:	William Garden Products Co., Ltd.
To:	Shanghai Qianjin International Forwarder Co., Ltd.
Attn:	Mr. Yu
Date:	March 17, 2019
Re:	Request for sea freight rate from Yiwu to Seattle

Dear Mr.Yu,

Please kindly provide your sea freight quatation from Yiwu, China to Seattle, U.S.A. I need transit time as well.

Commodity：wooden flower stands and wooden flower pots
Size of containers used：40' or 40' HQ
Volume：8 containers

Awaiting your early reply.

Best regards,
William
William Garden Products Co., Ltd.

图 2-1-3　客户威廉的海运询价邮件

2. Translate

请同学们帮助小余一起将图 2-1-3 所示的海运询价邮件翻译出来。

模块二 海 运

_____	:	William Garden Products Co., Ltd.
_____	:	Shanghai Qianjin International Forwarder Co., Ltd.
_____	:	Mr. Yu
_____	:	_____
_____	:	_____

Dear Mr.Yu,

_____:

Please kindly provide your sea freight quotation from Yiwu, China to Seattle, U.S.A. I need transit time as well.

Commodity： wooden flower stands and wooden flower pots

Size of containers used：40' or 40' HQ

Volume：8 containers

Awaiting your early reply.

Best regards,
William
William Garden Products Co., Ltd.

3. Answer

（1）这封询价邮件提及了哪些方面的内容？（用英文或中文回答均可）

（2）这封询价邮件是否遵循了四大要领？（用英文或中文回答均可）

二、实施海运邮件报价任务

现在，小余已经能读懂客户发来的海运询价邮件，在实施海运邮件报价之前，请先进入知识学苑（2-1-5）开展任务实施前的学习。

知识学苑（2-1-5）——海运邮件报价的典型句型

海运邮件报价一般出现在新客户报价中。与电话报价相比，邮件报价更注重言简意赅，但同时也要对新客户表示友好和强烈达成交易的意愿。

（一）细读询价，确认需求

1. We would appreciate if you can offer your best …（填写运费类别）rate from …（填写启运港）to …（填写目的港）

2. Commodity： …（填写运输的商品名称）
Size of containers used： …（填写集装箱规格）
Volume： …（整箱货中填写集装箱数量）

（二）开门见山，准备报价

1. Referring to your inquiry dated …（填写询价日期）for sea freight from …（填写启运港）to …（填写目的港）， please find our best …（填写运费类别）rate as follows（including PCS, BAF etc.）

2. We now list out the following rate guideline for your reference.

（三）报价完成，表示诚意

1. Should you have any other questions, please don't hesitate to contact us.
2. Please advise your comment on the rates.
3. We are looking forward to your confirmation / support soonest.
4. Awaiting your early reply.
5. Best regards.

（一）Read and Complete 读语句，选择正确词语

在海运邮件报价前，小余认真学习了海运邮件报价的典型句型。下面请从给定的词语中选择正确的单词进行填空。

on	from…to…	need	should	must
include	including	regards	date	dated
find	lookingforward	finds	lookforward	anyother
advise	asfollows	hesitate	referring	

（1）_____ to your inquiry _____ July 18, 2018 _____ sea freight _____ Shanghai, China _____ Beirut, Lebanon, please _____ our best all-in rate _____（_____ BAF, DDC etc.）

模块二 海　运

（2）Please_____your comment_____the rates.

（3）_____you have_____questions, please don't_____to contact me.

（4）We are_____to your confirmation.

（5）Best_____.

（二）Read and Translate 读函电，翻译往来邮件

小余向资深货代销售员老李学习，要来了老李与客户往来的海运询价、报价邮件，将相关函电整理出来，并利用空余时间将英文翻译为中文。

1. 翻译海运询价邮件（节选）

Re:	Sea freight rate inquiry

Dear Mr. Li,

We would appreciate if you can offer your best all-in rate from Shanghai, China to Beirut, Lebanon.

译文：_____

_____

_____

Commodity：footwear

Size of containers used：20' foot container

Volume：6 containers once every two months

译文：_____

_____

_____

Please respond today as our customer is waiting. Thanks in advance for your soonest reply.

译文：_____

_____

_____

Best regards,

Jacky Chan

Beirut SS Products I/E Co., Ltd.

译文：_____

_____

2. 翻译海运报价邮件（节选）

Reply:

MY Chan,
Referring to your inquiry dated August 27, 2018 for sea freight from Shanghai, China to Beirut, Lebanon, please find our best all-in rate as follows （including BAF，DDC etc.）
译文：_____
_____
_____

USD 2,200 / 20'
Carrier：COSCO
T/T：28days（direct vessel to Beirut）
Expected Time of Delivery：every working day
译文：_____
_____
_____

Please advise your comment on the rates. Should you have any other questions, please don't hesitate to contact us. We are looking forward to your confirmation.
译文：_____
_____
_____

Best regards,
Mr. Li
Shanghai Qianjin International Forwarder Co.,Ltd.
译文：_____
_____
_____

（三）Read and Write 读询价，实施邮件报价

通过向老李学习，小余细致分析了新客户威廉先生的各方面需求，在经过仔细查询和认真确认后，拟定了如下海运邮件报价的中文提纲。

1. 拟定海运报价邮件中文提纲

Reply:

亲爱的威廉先生：

  关于你方 2019 年 3 月 17 日来函询问的，从中国义乌到美国西雅图的海运运费报价，为您提供我们最优惠的海运包干费率如下：

义乌至宁波的拖柜费：2 400 RMB / 40 英尺柜或 40 英尺高柜

报关费：100 RMB / 票

订舱费：340 RMB / 40 英尺柜

     430 RMB / 40 英尺高柜

海运费：3 400 美元 / 40 英尺柜或 40 英尺高柜（已包括燃油附加费、目的港交货费等）

承运人：东方海外货柜航运公司

运输频率：每周六出发

运输时间：17 天到达

请对费率提出您的意见。如果您有其他问题，请马上与我们联系。我们期待您能尽早订舱。

此致

敬礼

小余
上海前进国际货代公司

2. 撰写海运报价英文邮件

Reply:

【知识检测】

"海运邮件报价"这一任务的评价采用自测形式,请学生在实施任务后对于应掌握的词汇或句型进行回顾,完成 Self-check,对于已掌握的,在它前面的括号中打"√",完成表 2-1-4 的填写。

表 2-1-4　海运邮件报价知识自测表

Self-check		
I learned:		
(　) sea freight rates	(　) the name of the commodity	(　) frequency
(　) shipping spaces	(　) preferred mode of transport/carrier	(　) origin port
(　) destination port	(　) the weight of the commodity	(　) transit time
(　) the volume of the commodity	(　) the dimension of the commodity	
(　) We would appreciate if you can offer your best … rate from … to …		
(　) Commodity：…		
(　) Size of containers used：…		
(　) Volume：…		
(　) Referring to your inquiry dated … for sea freight from … to …, please find our best … rate as follows（including PCS, BAF etc.）		
(　) We now list out the following rate guideline for your reference.		
(　) Should you have any other questions, please don't hesitate to contact us.		
(　) Please advise your comment on the rates.		
(　) We are looking forward to your confirmation / support soonest.		
(　) Awaiting your early reply.		
(　) Best regards.		
I can:		
(　) make sea quotation by mail.		

项目二 海运操作

Project Two Sea Freight Operation

【学习目标】

1. 能认识海运主要港口、航线、公司的名称及其缩写。
2. 能阅读海运日常操作的往来函电。
3. 在学习海运操作的过程中,培养严谨求实的职业习惯。

Task One Major Shipping Ports, Routes and Companies

任务一 认识海运主要港口、航线和公司

【任务导入】

小余在向师傅老李学习办理业务的过程中,发现老李和客户谈的许多港口和航线,他都一无所知。老李告诉小余,熟悉海运主要港口、航线和船公司,了解有哪些航线的船舶会在此经过,可以帮助货代员快速有效地规划出既省时又节约成本的方案,并体现出货代员的专业性,这也是一个合格的货代员必须具备的职业素养和能力。因此,小余准备恶补一下这方面的知识。

请与小余一起认识下海运主要港口、航线和船公司吧!

【任务实施】

一、认识海运主要航线和港口

请先进入知识学苑(2-2-1)开展任务实施前的学习,认识海运主要航线和港口。

知识学苑（2-2-1）——海运主要航线及其基本港

（一）目前世界海运主要的集装箱航线：

远东—北美航线（Asia-North America）

远东—欧洲、地中海航线（Asia- North Europe and Mediterranean）

北美—欧洲、地中海航线（North America- North Europe and Mediterranean）

（二）中国主要的海运航线

近洋航线：

航线名称		主要基本港名称
近洋航线	港澳线	香港（HONGKONG）、澳门（MACAO）
	新马线	新加坡（SINGAPORE），马来西亚（MALAYSIA）的巴生港（PORTKELANG）、槟城（PENANG）和马六甲（MALACEA）等
	暹罗湾线	越南（VIETNAM）的海防（HAIPHONG），泰国的曼谷（BANGKOK）等
	科伦坡，孟加拉湾线	斯里兰卡（SRI LANKA）的科伦坡（COLOMBO），孟加拉（BANGLADESH）的吉大港（CHITTAGONG），印度（INDIA）的加尔各答（CHENNA CALCUTTA）等
	菲律宾线	菲律宾（THE PHILIPPINES）的马尼拉港（MANILA）
	印度尼西亚线	印度尼西亚（INDONESIA）的雅加达（JAKARTA）、三宝垄（SEMARANG）等
	澳大利亚新西兰线	澳大利亚（AUSTRALIA）的悉尼（SYDNEY）、墨尔本（MELBOURNE）、布里斯班（BRISBANE），新西兰的奥克兰（AUCKLAND）、惠灵顿（WELLINGTON）等
	巴布亚新几内亚线	巴布亚新几内亚（PAPUA NEW GUINEA）的莱城（LAE）、莫尔兹比港（PORT MORESBY）
	日本线	日本（JAPAN）的神户（KOBE）、大阪（OSAKA）、名古屋（NAGOYA）和横滨（YOKOHAMA）等
	韩国线	韩国（KOREAN）的釜山（BUSAN）、仁川（INCHON）等
	波斯湾线	巴基斯坦（PAKISTAN）的卡拉奇（KARACHI），伊朗（IRAN）的阿巴斯（BANDAR ABBAS），科威特的科威特港（KUWAIT），阿联酋（UNITED ARAB EMIRATES）的迪拜（DUBAI）
	地中海线	地中海东部： 黎巴嫩（LEBANON）的贝鲁特（BEIRUT），以色列（ISRAEL）的海法（HAIFA），叙利亚（SYRIA）的拉塔基亚（LATTAKIA）。 地中海南部： 埃及（EGYPT）的塞得港（PORT SAID）、亚历山大（ALEXANDRIA），阿尔及利亚(ALGERIA)的阿尔及尔（ALGIERS）。 地中海北部： 意大利（ITALY）的热那亚（GENOVA），西班牙（SPAIN）的巴塞罗那（BARCELONA）等

续表

航线名称		主要基本港名称
近洋航线	西北欧线	比利时（BELGIUM）的安特卫普（ANTWERP），荷兰（THE NETHERLANDS）的鹿特丹（ROTTERDAM），德国（GERMANY）的汉堡（HAMBURG）、不来梅（BREMEN），法国（FRANCE）的勒弗尔（LE HAVRE），英国（UK）的伦敦（LONDON）、利物浦（LIVERPOOL），丹麦（DENMARK）的哥本哈根（COPENHAGEN），挪威的奥斯陆（OSLO），瑞典（SWEDEN）的斯德哥尔摩（STOCKHOLM）、哥德堡（GOTHENBURG），芬兰（FINLAND）的赫尔辛基（HELSINKI）等
	美国加拿大航线	加拿大（CANADA）的温哥华（VANCOUVER）、蒙特利尔（MONTREAL）、多伦多（TORONTO），美国（THE UNITED STATES）的西雅图（SEATTLE）、旧金山（SAN FRANCISCO）、洛杉矶（LOS ANGELES）、纽约（NEW YORK）、波士顿（BOSTON）、费城（PHILADELPHIA）、巴尔的摩（BALTIMORE）等
	南美洲西岸线	秘鲁（PERU）的卡亚俄（CALLAO），智利（CHILE）的阿里卡（ARICA）、瓦尔帕莱索（VALPARAISO）等

（三）中国部分海运港口

港口名称	港口代码
上海港 SHANGHAI	CNSHA
宁波港 NINGBO	CNNGB
深圳港 SHENZHEN	CNSZX
广州港 GUANGZHOU	CNCAN
青岛港 QINGDAO	CNTAO
天津港 TIANJIN	CNTNJ
厦门港 XIAMEN	CNXMN
大连港 DALIAN	CNDLC
营口港 YINGKOU	CNYIK
连云港 LIANYUNGANG	CNLYG

（一）Read and Match 读词汇，匹配港口名称

在"知识学苑"中学习了海运的主要航线和港口后，小余很想检验自己的学习成果。他需要熟读这些港口的英文名称，并与它的中文名称、所属国家匹配起来，如图 2-2-1 所示。

港口中文名称	港口英文名称	所属国家
神户巷	BRISBANE	JAPAN
洛杉矶港	ANTWERP	UNITED STATES
温哥华港	VANCOUVER	CANADA
布里斯班港	KOBE	AUSTRALIA
安特卫普港	LOS ANGELES	BEIGIUM
鹿特丹港	DUBAI	SINGAPORE
新加坡港	SINGAPORE	GERMANY
迪拜港	ROTTERDAM	THE UNITED ARAB EMIRATES
巴生港	HAMBURG	NETHERLANDS
汉堡港	PORT KELANG	MALAYSIA

图 2-2-1 世界著名港口连连看

（二）Choose and Complete 做选择，完成表格填写

小余不仅要了解港口的名称和地理位置，也要了解这些基本港所在的海运航线，以便更好地帮助客户规划运输方案。请将以下港口匹配到相应航线中，填写表 2-2-1。

A. OSAKA（大阪）　　　　　　B. BARCELONA（巴塞罗那）

C. PORT KELANG（巴生）　　　D. MONTREAL（蒙特利尔）

E. ROTTERDAM（鹿特丹）　　　F. SYDNEY（悉尼）

G. PHILADELPHIA（费城）　　　H. AUCKLAND（奥克兰）

I. NAGOYA（名古屋）　　　　　J. PENANG（槟城）

K. KOBE（神户）　　　　　　　L. ANTWERP（安特卫普）

M. TORONTO（多伦多）　　　　N. ALEXANDRIA（亚历山大）

O. HAMBURG（汉堡）　　　　　P. MALACEA（马六甲）

Q. SAN FRANCISCO（旧金山）　　R. COPENHAGEN（哥本哈根）

S. VALPARAISO（瓦尔帕莱索）　　T. BRISBANE（布里斯班）

U. GENOVA（热那亚）

表 2-2-1　海运航线—港口匹配表

航线名称	基本港口名称
中国—新马航线	
中国—澳大利亚新西兰航线	
中国—日本航线	
中国—地中海线	
中国—西北欧航线	
中国—美国加拿大航线	
中国—南美洲航线	

二、认识中外主要海运公司

请先进入知识学苑（2-2-2）开展任务实施前的准备，认识中国及世界主要海运公司。

知识学苑（2-2-2）——中外主要海运公司					
序号	图标	公司	简称	缩写	所属
1	MAERSK SEALAND	马士基航运有限公司	马士基	MAERSK	丹麦
2	msc	地中海航运公司	地中海航运	MSC	瑞士
3	COSCO	中远物流有限公司	中远海运	COSCO	中国
4	CMA CGM	达飞轮船有限公司	达飞轮船	CMA	法国
5	Hapag-Lloyd	德国赫伯罗特轮船公司	赫伯罗特	HAPAG-LLOYD	德国

续表

序号	图标	公司	简称	缩写	所属
6		Ocean Network Express	海洋网联	ONE	日本
7		长荣海运股份有限公司	长荣海运	EMC	中国台湾
8		阳明海运有限公司	阳明海运	YML	中国台湾
9		现代商船株式会社	现代商船	HMM	韩国
10		太平船务有限公司	太平船务	PIL	新加坡
11		以星综合航运有限公司	以星航运	ZIM	以色列
12		万海航运股份有限公司	万海航运	WANHAI	中国台湾
13		中谷海运集团	中谷海运	ZHONGGU	中国
14		高丽海运株式会社	高丽海运	KMTC	韩国
15		伊朗伊斯兰航运公司	伊朗航运	IRISL	伊朗

模块二 海 运

（一）Choose and Match 做选择，完成连线匹配

小余为了更好、更快地熟悉船公司名称及其缩写代码，将以上船公司的名称和代码进行混合，如图 2-2-2 所示，帮小余快速地连线完成匹配吧。

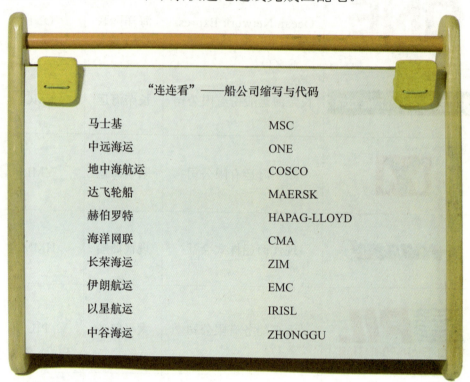

"连连看"——船公司缩写与代码

马士基	MSC
中远海运	ONE
地中海航运	COSCO
达飞轮船	MAERSK
赫伯罗特	HAPAG-LLOYD
海洋网联	CMA
长荣海运	ZIM
伊朗航运	EMC
以星航运	IRISL
中谷海运	ZHONGGU

图 2-2-2　船公司名称代码匹配

（二）Read and Judge 读短文，完成判断

如何选择最合适的航运公司，小余犯了难。请阅读以下短文，了解选择航运公司的小技巧，在正确的表述前打"√"。

1. Read

Five Tips When Selecting a Cargo Shipping Company

You're ready to make your shipment. Here is a top five of tips to take into consideration when choosing a cargo shipping company.

Tip # 1: Check the Cargo Shipping Company's Registration and Licensing

An important factor is to make sure your cargo shipping company is fully reliable and trustworthy. Check out their registration and licensing and compare.

Tip # 2: Cargo Loading Services

When searching for the best company to move your items, ask about the loading services offered. One of the most popular is known as door to door shipping.

Tip # 3: Variety of Container Size and Capacity

Depending on what you want to ship and what you can leave behind will determine what size container will be needed for your move.

Tip # 4: Cargo Tracking Tools

Whether you're given an online code to see where your ship is in transit or you receive emails updating you on your item's travels, you'll want to ask about this tracking option.

Tip # 5: The Overall Price

Always compare the overall price of the items shipped and ask about fees such as fuel, insurance, tracking etc. Hidden fees should be made available to you.

【参考译文】

选择航运公司的五个技巧

你已经准备要装运了。以下是选择航运公司时要考虑的五大建议：

技巧1：查看航运公司的注册和许可证

查看并比较航运公司的注册信息和许可证，确保航运公司的可靠性。

技巧2：货物装卸服务

咨询航运公司提供的装卸服务，其中最受欢迎的是门到门运输。

技巧3：多尺寸、多类型的集装箱

根据运输的货物确定集装箱的类型和大小。

技巧4：货物跟踪工具

无论您是通过密码在线查看您的船在运输途中的位置，还是收到更新邮件，您都希望有这项跟踪服务。

技巧5：看全包价

询问燃料、保险、跟踪等费用，确定比较的是全包运费。隐藏费用应告知于你。

2. Judge

☐ (1) One of the most important thing is to check your shipping company's registration and licensing.

☐ (2) It's not necessary to ask about the loading services when searching for the shipping company.

☐ (3) You need to figure out whether the price of the items shipped includes some hidden fees.

☐ (4) When choosing a shipping company, you can compare its registration, licensing, services and price.

模块二 海 运

【知识检测】

"认识海运主要港口、航线和公司"这一任务的评价采用自测形式,请学生在实施任务后对于应掌握的词汇或句型进行回顾,完成 Self-check,对于已掌握的,在它前面的括号中打"√",完成表 2-2-2 的填写。

表 2-2-2 海运港口、航线与公司知识自测表

Self-check		
I learned:		
( ) CHINA PORTS	( ) LOS ANGELES	( ) VANCOUVER
( ) BRISBANE	( ) ANTWERP	( ) ROTTERDAM
( ) SINGAPORE	( ) DUBAI	( ) PORT KELANG
( ) HAMBURG	( ) MSC	( ) ONE
( ) COSCO	( ) MAERSK	( ) HAPAG-LLOYD
( ) CMA	( ) ZIM	( ) EMC
( ) IRISL	( ) ZHONGGU	
I can:		
( ) recognize shipping ports, routes and companies		
( ) retell tips to select a cargo shipping company		

Task Two Shipping Correspondence Reading
任务二 阅读海运操作函电

【任务导入】

操作部的货代新人小方发现师傅老陈通常用电子邮件和传真与国外客户洽谈业务。这不仅简便快捷,而且不受时差影响,也方便回看、查阅、跟踪落实每笔业务的进度,还可作为洽谈交流的凭证。

可是当他阅读师傅的往来邮件时,发现邮件虽然简短,但是使用了非常多的缩略语和专业术语,常常让他看得不明所以。原来,操作员在和熟悉的老客户交流时,常常会

使用一些双方都理解的缩略语和术语，以便提高沟通效率和便捷度。

让我们和小方一起去学习货代员常用的缩写和术语，读懂海运操作函电吧！

【任务实施】

一、明确海运操作函电的基本格式

请先进入知识学苑（2-2-3）开展任务实施前的学习，认识海运操作函电的基本格式。

知识学苑（2-2-3）——海运操作函电的基本格式

用电子邮件方式传送的海运函电，其基本格式与商业书信相似，一般有以下几个部分：

（一）**信头（Header）**

FM (From): 发件人

Date: 发件时间

To: 收件人

Cc: 副本抄送

Bcc (Blind Cc): 密送

Sub (Subject)：邮件主题或事由

Re (Reply): 回复

FW (Forward): 转发

Attachment: 附件

Attn (Attention): 经办人

（二）**正文（Body）**

电子邮件的正文一般包括以下几个部分：

1. 称呼 (Salutation)

电子邮件一般使用非正式的称呼，同辈或同事间可以直呼其名，对长辈或上级最好使用头衔加上姓，例如：Dear Johnson; Dear Madam/Sir; Hi, Davis 等。

2. 主文 (Body of the Letter)

涉外电子邮件的正文书写通常采用齐头式，即指正文各部分都从每行的左边开始。

3. 结束语 (Complimentary Close)

结尾的致意可根据双方关系选择合适的词句。常用但非正式的致意有：Best regards, Regards, Best wishes, Have a nice day, Good day to you, Sincerely yours, Sincerely 等。

4. 签名 (Signature)

写信人的署名，可包括姓名、写信人职务及部门、公司、公司地址 (Add.)、电话 (Tel.)、传真 (Fax.)、电子邮件地址 (E-mail) 等信息。

模块二 海 运

（一）Think and Match 读词汇，匹配格式名称

在"知识学苑"中学习了海运函电的基本格式之后，小方了解了海运函电的撰写格式，特别是信头部分的功能和缩写给他留下了深刻的印象。他尝试将信头部分的缩写与其中文名称匹配起来，如图 2-2-3 所示。

图 2-2-3 信头部分缩写匹配

（二）Read and Complete 读邮件，完成邮件填空

在了解了海运函电的基本格式之后，资深货代员老陈将一份拟好的货运报价邮件正文交给小方，让他补充完相应内容，发送给国外客户 Chris，并抄送给 Emily。和小方一起来完成这个任务吧！

```
A. To
B. FM
C. Date
D. Cc
E. Re
```

_____: Michael Chen

_____: Chris

_____: Emily

_____: Aug. 21, 2020

F. Subject: _____ : Rate update ex. SHA to LGB

Dear Chris,

Referring to your enquiry dated Aug. 20 for sea freight from SHA to LGB, please find our best all-in rate as follows:

USD2,015/40'HQ

USD1,615/20'

Carrier: MSC

T/T: 15 days (direct vessel to Long Beach)

ETD: every Fri.

Advise your comment on the rates. Should you have other questions, please feel free to contact me.

Best Regards,

Michael Chen

二、读写海运操作函电

请先进入知识学苑（2-2-4）开展任务实施前的准备，学习海运操作函电的常用表达。

知识学苑（2-2-4）——海运操作函电的常用表达

在实际业务操作中，海运函电通常使用一些单词的简写，以提高沟通语言的简洁性。这些缩略语通常是在沟通双方均能理解的情况下使用的。部分常用的表达方式如下：

ABV: above 以上
ACPTG: accepting 接受
ADV.: advise 通知、告知意见
ADVD: advised 通知、告知
ASAP: as soon as possible 尽快
B4: before 在……之前
BCZ: because 因为
BKG: booking 预定
CBMS: cubic meters 立方米
CFMD: confirmed 确认
CGO: cargo 货物
CK: check 检查
CKG: checking 检查
CMBN: combine 合并
CNCTG: connecting 连接
CNEE: consignee 收货人
CTNS: cartons 纸箱
CUD: could 可以
DESCRIP.: description 货品描述
DIFF: different 不同的
ETA: established time of arrival 预计到港时间
ETD: established time of departure 预计离港时间
FCL: full container load 整箱、整柜（整集装箱，与LCL相对）
FCTY: factory 工厂
FDR: feeder 驳船（与vessel相对）
FR: for 关于
FYI: for your information 供你参考
HV: have
HWVR: however 然而
I/O: instead of 代替
INFO: information 信息

KGS: kilograms 千克
L/C#: letter of credit number 信用证编号
LCL: less than container load 拼箱（与FCL相对）
MLB: mini land bridge 小路桥运输
N: and 和
ND: need 需要
PCS: pieces 件数
PLND: planed 计划
PLS: please 请
PO#: purchase order number 采购号
RCVD: received 接收
RDY: ready 备好货时间
RE: about 关于、事由
RE-CFM: reconfirm 再次确认
RGDS: regards 致意
RYF: Re your fax 回复您的传真
SHP: ship 运输
SHPG: shipping 运输
SLG: sailing 起航
STY#: stock yard number 仓库编号
TDY: today 今天
THKS: thanks 谢谢
THS 4 YR HELP: thanks for your help 感谢你的帮助
TTL: total 总共
U: you 你
VNDR: vender 卖方
VSL: vessel 货船
W/: with 和
WIL: will 将要
WUD: would 会；要
WUDN'T: wouldn't 不会

典型句型如下：

（一）开篇写明事由，使对方一目了然这封邮件是答复哪一封邮件的

1. RE NEW BKG FR ××× FOB QINGDAO TO KOBE

就客户×××新的 FOB 货，从青岛到神户订舱信息。

2. RE ××× BKG/FOB QINGDAO TO KOBE

就客户×××的 FOB 货，从青岛到神户订舱信息。

3. RYF 8/20, ×××/KOBE PO# 12345/11.6 CBM N PUSAN PO# 67891/7.80 CBM…

就你 8 月 20 日传真，×××收货人 / 到神户 / 采购号 12345/11.6 立方米和到釜山 / 采购号 67891/7.80 立方米……

4. RE UPDATED RATES EX CHINA PORTS TO MED. PORTS.

关于更新从中国到地中海的运价。

（二）简明扼要说清自己要表达的意思

1. PLAN TO SHIP LCL VIA MSC DIRECT VSL "MAERSK SHEERNESS V. 1014" SLG NBO ON 12/14. ETA LAX 12/26. ETA OAK 12/28. RATE/NBO-OAK: US $115/CMB.

计划出运拼箱，通过地中海船公司直航服务，船名"MAERSK SHEERNESS"航次"1014"，12 月 14 日驶离宁波，预计 12 月 26 日到洛杉矶，12 月 26 日到奥克兰。运价每立方米 115 美金。

2. PLAN TO SHIP ON FDR "SEA BRIGHT V. 9635" SLG QIN 7/16, CNCTG MAIN VSL "CALIFORNIA ZUES V. 69" W/ETD KOBE 8/2. ETA LAX 8/13.

计划使用"SEA BRIGHT V. 9635"驳船，7 月 16 日从青岛出发，连接大船"CALIFORNIA ZUES V. 69"，8 月 2 日从神户出发，8 月 13 日到达洛杉矶。

（三）结束语简短

PLS ADVISE. 请告知意见。

PLS ADV ASAP. 请尽快告知意见。

THKS & RGDS. 感谢和问候！

PLS CFM. 请确认。

TKS 4 YR HELP. 感谢您的帮助。

（一）Write and Match 写一写，匹配缩略语

在知识学苑中学习了海运操作函电中的一些常见词汇表达后，小方读函电顺畅了很多。他为了更快地熟悉这些词汇表达，摘录出了一部分，尝试将常用词与其缩略语进行匹配。

1. Write

请在横线上写出以下词汇的缩略语

模块二 海 运

（　　　　）= booking（订舱）
（　　　　）= for（关于）
（　　　　）= from（从……起）
（　　　　）= vender（卖方）
（　　　　）= purchase order number（采购单号）
（　　　　）= stock yard number（仓库编号）
（　　　　）= cartons（纸箱）
（　　　　）= pieces（件数）
（　　　　）= cubic meter（立方米）
（　　　　）= description（货品描述）
（　　　　）= letter of credit number（信用证编号）
（　　　　）= kilograms（千克）
（　　　　）= ready（备好货时间）
（　　　　）= feeder（驳船）
（　　　　）= vessel（货船）
（　　　　）= less than container load（拼箱）
（　　　　）= full container load（整箱、整柜）
（　　　　）= sailing（起航）
（　　　　）= connecting（连接）
（　　　　）= with（和）
（　　　　）= established time of arrival（预计到港时间）
（　　　　）= established time of departure（预计离港时间）
（　　　　）= please（请）
（　　　　）= advise（告知意见，通知）
（　　　　）= thanks（谢谢）
（　　　　）= regards（致意）

2. Match

将合适的缩略语填写到横线上，把句子补充完整。

| BKG | 4 | ETA | ASAP | RYF |
| RGDS | SLG | CMB | VSL | CFM |

（1）RE NEW ＿＿＿＿＿ FR ××× FOB QINGDAO TO KOBE.

（2）＿＿＿＿＿ 8/20, ×××/KOBE PO# 12345/11.6 CBM.

（3）PLAN TO SHIP LCL VIA MSC DIRECT ＿＿＿＿＿ "MAERSK SHEERNESS V. 1014" ＿＿＿＿＿ NBO ON 12/14. ＿＿＿＿＿ LAX 12/26. ETA OAK 12/28. RATE/NBO-OAK: US $115/＿＿＿＿＿.

84

（4）PLS ADV _____.

（5）TKS _____ YR HELP.

（6）PLS _____.

（7）THKS & _____.

（二）Read and Translate 读邮件，翻译主要内容

在了解了海运操作函电常用的一些缩略语和表达方式后，小方以师傅老陈的业务函电作为学习素材，阅读并翻译海运函电，以期更快地读懂掌握。

FM: Michael Chen (Shanghai)
To: Robert (USA)
Date: DEC.4
Subject：RE NEW BKG FR ××× FM LYG TO LGB
DEAR ROBERT,
RE NEW BKG FR ××× FOB LYG TO LGB
VENDER　PO#　　SKY#　　CTNS　　PCS　　DESCRIP.L/C#　　KGS　　CBM　　RDY
PMS　　　12345　1234567　140　　50,042　TOY TRUCKS　　1,234　　11.6　　12/12 PMS　　　22345　2276543　150　　2,784　LEATHER COATS　2,345　　11.5　　12/11
PLAN TO COMBINE ABOVE CARGO IN 1×20' TO SHIP ON FDR "PUHAI229 V. B1535E" SLG LYG 12/15, CNCTG MAIN VSL "CALIFORNIA ZUES V. 69" W/ETD TAO 12/17. ETA LGB 12/25. PLS ADV. 　THKS & RGDS. 　MICHAEL CHEN

1. Mark and Circle 圈一圈，标记缩略语

将此封函电中的缩略语圈出，并摘录在下方横线上，注明其中文名称。

_____

_____

_____

_____

_____

模块二 海 运

2. Read and Translate 读函电，翻译函电

（1）RE NEW BKG FR XXX FOB LYG TO LGB

译文：_____

（2）

VENDER	PO#	SKU#	CTNS	PCS	DESCRIP.L/C#	KGS	CBM	RDY
RMS	12345	1234567	140	50,042	TOY TRUCKS	1,234	11.6	12/12

译文：_____

（3）PLAN TO COMBINE ABOVE CARGO IN 1×20' TO SHIP ON FDR "PUHAI229 V. B1535E" SLG LYG 12/15, CNCTG MAIN VSL "CALIFORNIA ZUES V. 69" W/ETD TAO 12/17. ETA LGB 12/25. PLS ADV.

译文：_____

（4）THKS & RGDS.

译文：_____

（三）Write and Complete 写一写，把函电补充完整

师傅老陈把国外货代回复的邮件找出来给小方学习，邮件内容如下：

FM ROBERT TO MICHAEL CHEN

RE ××× BKG/FOB LYG …CNEE CFMD OK TO CMBN PO# 12345 W/PO#22345 FR TTL 23.1 CBMS TO SHIP IN 1×20' TO LGB, HWVR CNEE ADVD THEY REALLY NEED A VSL W/EARLIER ETA THAN CALIF.ZUES V. 69. PLS CK W/OTHER CARRIERS N ADV IF ANY WILL HAVE A VSL W/EARLIER ETA LGB … IF NOT, CNEE ADV OK TO SHP AS YOU MENTIONED ABOVE.

【参考译文】

就客户×××的FOB货，从连云港到长滩的订舱信息。收货人同意把采购号12345和采购号22345两票货合并，总共23.1立方米，用一个20尺柜出运到长滩。但是收货人通知说他们需要一艘早于"CALIF.ZUES V.69"到港时间的船。请查看其他运输公司，若有任何能提前抵达长滩的船请通知。如果没有，收货人通知同意按您说的方案运输。

1. Read and Complete 读一读，把函电补充完整

师傅老陈为了让小方更好地熟悉缩略语的使用，这次他卖了个关子，将邮件中的部分词汇隐去，看看小方是否能补全邮件。请和小方一起在横线上填写缺失的词汇缩略语吧。

FM ROBERT TO MICHAEL CHEN

_____(1)_____（关于）×××BKG/FOB LYG ..._____(2)_____（收货人）CFMD OK TO_____(3)_____（合并）PO# 12345 W/PO#22345 FR_____(4)_____（总共）23.1 _____(5)_____（立方米）TO SHIP IN 1×20' TO LGB, HWVR CNEE ADVD THEY REALLY NEED A VSL W/EARLIER_____(6)_____（预计到港时间）THAN CALIF.ZUES V.69. _____(7)_____（请）CK W/OTHER CARRIERS N_____(8)_____（告知）IF ANY WILL HAVE A VSL W/EARLIER ETA LGB ... IF NOT, CNEE ADV OK TO_____(9)_____（运输）AS YOU MENTIONED ABOVE.

2. Translate and Write 译一译，练习函电撰写

在学习完以上两封海运函电后，师傅老陈告诉小方，12月17日从青岛出发的船"CALIF.ZUES V.69"是我们可以找到的最快发出的船，所以将会就此船订舱。请小方根据以上信息，草拟一份回函交给师傅审核。和小方一起试一试吧。

FM MICHAEL CHEN TO ROBERT

RE_____

_____

_____

参考答案：

RE ×××BKG/FOB LYG ... "CALIF.ZUES V.69" SLG TAO 12/17 IS THE FASTEST VSL WE CAN FIND. SO WIL BK SPACE ON THIS VSL.

【知识检测】

"阅读海运操作函电"这一任务的评价采用自测形式，请学生在实施任务后对于应掌握的词汇、句型和表达进行回顾，完成Self-check，对于已掌握的，在它前面的括号中打"√"，完成表2-2-3的填写。

模块二 海 运

表 2-2-3 阅读海运操作函电知识自测表

Self-check		
I learned:		
a. basic mail format:		
(　) FM	(　) TO	(　) CC
(　) BCC	(　) ATTN	(　) RE
(　) FW	(　) SUB	(　) ATTACHMENT
b. some abbreviations in shipping correspondences:		
(　) BK	(　) FR	(　) FM
(　) VNDN	(　) PO#	(　) STY#
(　) CTNS	(　) PICS	(　) CBMS
(　) DESCRIP.	(　) L/C#	(　) KGS
(　) RDY	(　) FDR	(　) VSL
(　) LCL	(　) FCL	(　) SLG
(　) CNCTG	(　) W/	(　) ETA
(　) ETD	(　) PLS	(　) ADV
(　) THKS	(　) RGDS	
c. some sentences in shipping correspondences:		
(　) RE NEW BKG FR ××× FOB QINGDAO TO KOBE		
(　) RE ××× BKG/FOB QINGDAO TO KOBE		
(　) RYF 8/20, ×××/KOBE PO# 12345/11.6 CBM N PUSAN PO# 67891/7.80 CBM…		
(　) PLAN TO SHIP LCL VIA MSC DIRECT VSL "MAERSK SHEERNESS V. 1014" SLG NBO ON 12/14. ETA LAX 12/26. ETA OAK 12/28. RATE/NBO-OAK: US $115/CMB.		
(　) PLAN TO SHIP ON FDR "SEA BRIGHT V. 9635" SLG QIN 7/16, CNCTG MAIN VSL "CALIFORNIA ZUES V. 69" W/ETD KOBE 8/2. ETA LAX 8/13.		
(　) PLS ADVISE		
(　) THKS & RGDS.		
I can:		
(　) read and comprehend shipping correspondences.		

Module Three Air Freight Transport

模块三 空 运

项目一 空运报价

Project One Air Quotations

【学习目标】

1. 能沟通完成空运电话报价。
2. 能阅读客户的空运询价邮件，并撰写空运报价邮件。
3. 在学习空运报价的过程中，培养严谨求实的职业习惯。

Task One Air E-mail Quotation
任务一 空运电话报价

【任务导入】

小余是上海前进国际货代公司的实习销售人员。最近与公司长期合作的老客户——杰克先生准备打电话向小余进行空运运费的询价。刚上岗的货代新人小余十分焦虑，担心无法与杰克先生顺畅地沟通。

请帮助小余一起完成空运电话报价吧！

【任务实施】

一、明确空运报价要素

请先进入知识学苑（3-1-1）开展任务实施前的学习，认识常见的空运运费种类。

> 知识学苑（3-1-1）——常见的空运运费种类
>
> 空运报价中涵盖了主要空运运价和空运附加费，以下为部分重要空运运费种类。
>
> （一）主要空运运价
> 1. GCR = General Cargo Rates——普通货物运价
> 2. CCR = Commodity Classification Rate——等级货物运价
> 3. SCR = Specific Commodity Rates——特种货物运价
> 4. UCR = Unitized Consignments Rate——集装箱货物运价
>
> （二）空运附加费
> 1. ATC = Air Terminal Charge——机场费
> 2. ABF = Airway Bill Fee——空运提单费
> 3. FSC = Fuel Surcharge——燃油附加费
> 4. SCC = Security Sur Charge——空运提单费
> 5. D/O fee——换单费
> 6. Waiting Charge——待时费
> 7. Customs Inspection Fee——海关查验费
> 8. Container Loading Charge——内装箱费
> 9. Customs clearance Fee——报关费
> 10. I/E Bonded Charge——转境费/过境费

（一）Think and Match 读词汇，匹配费用名称

在"知识学苑"中学习了常见空运运价种类及空运附加费后，小余尝试将每项常见空运运价及相关费用的英文全称或英文缩写与它的中文名称进行匹配。

如图 3-1-1 所示，请将空运运价及费用的英文表述与中文表述进行正确连线。

图 3-1-1　常见空运附加费中英文配对

模块三　空　运

二、学习空运电话报价句型

在上一模块中，我们学习了海运电话报价，还记得五度准则吗？在进入空运电话报价前，请先进入知识学苑（3-1-2）开展实施任务前的学习，一起来和小余回忆下电话报价的重点句型吧！

知识学苑（3-1-2）—空运电话报价的重点句型
空运电话报价基本用语和海运电话报价类似，再来回顾下电话报价的通用句型及重点句型。 1. I would like to have…shipped from …to … 2. Can you make me an air quotation for …? 3. Please let me know the frequency and the transit time. 4. How many containers are used and what size? 5. Our air freight rate is … , including … 6. The … charge is … 7. I'll call you when I've made my decision. 8. I'm looking forward to your early reply.

（一）Read and Translate 读对话，翻译电话报价

师傅老李一直帮助小余学习货代销售知识，认真的小余将老李的空运电话报价实录整理出来，并利用空余时间将英文翻译为中文。

Mr. Li: Hello! This is Shanghai Qianjin International Forwarder Co., Ltd. Can I help you?

译文：_____

Michael: I would like to have some precision instruments shipped from Hangzhou, China to Yokohama, Japan. Can you make me an air quotation for DOOR TO PORT shipment?

译文：_____

Mr. Li: Sure. What do the instruments weigh?

译文：_____

Michael: 115 kilos.

译文：_____

Mr. Li: Do you know the size?

译文：_____

Michael：2 cubic meters. Can you offer me a rate?

译文：_____

Mr. Li: Sorry to keep you waiting. Hangzhou Customs clearance charge is 50 USD per shipment. The quarantine inspection charge is 0.01 USD for a carton. Our air freight rate is 3.1 USD a kilo. The pickup and delivery charge at destination is 100 USD. The destination

Customs clearance charge is 130 USD per shipment. The local Customs duties and taxes is 180 USD. The carrier is China Northwest Airlines.

译文：_____
_____
_____
_____

Michael: How about the transit time?

译文：_____

Mr. Li: This air transport would take 4 days.

译文：_____

Michael: I've got it. Thank you, and I'll call you when I've made my decision.

译文：_____

Mr. Li: I'm looking forward to your early reply.

译文：_____

（二）Remember and Complete 忆句型，补全电话报价

为了巩固学习成果，小余反复研究老李的电话报价实录，努力记忆空运电话报价的典型句型，并在以下横线上填写缺失的部分词汇。

Mr. Li：Hello!_____ _____Shanghai Qianjin International Forwarder Co., Ltd. Can I help you?

Michael: I would like to_____some precision instruments_____ _____Hangzhou, China_____Yokohama, Japan. Can you_____me a_____ _____for DOOR TO PORT shipment?

Mr. Li：What do the_____?

Michael：115 kilos.

Mr. Li：Do you know the size?

Michael：2 cubic meters. Can you_____me_____?

Mr. Li：_____is 50 USD per shipment. The_____is 0.01 USD for a carton. Our_____is 3.1 USD a kilo. The_____at destination is 100 USD. The destination _____is 130 USD per shipment. The local Customs duties and taxes is 180 USD. The carrier is China Northwest Airlines.

Michael：How about the transit time?

Mr. Li：This air transport_____ _____4 days.

Michael：I've_____it. Thank you, and I'll call you when I've_____ _____

decision.

Mr. Li: I'm_____ _____to your early reply.

三、实施空运电话报价任务

请先进入知识学苑（3-1-3）开展任务实施前的准备，学习我国参与国际空运涉及的主要航线和对应的航空公司。

知识学苑（3-1-3）——中国参与涉及的主要空运航线与航空公司	
主要空运航线	主要航空公司
北美航线	美国航空公司（American Airlines） 美国大陆航空公司（Continental Airlines） 美国西北航空公司（Northwest Airlines） 美国联合航空公司（United Airlines） 美国联邦航空公司（Federal Express） 美国维珍航空公司（Virgin Atlantic） 美国联合包裹运送公司（UPS） 加拿大航空公司（Canadian Airlines） 加拿大航空公司（Air Canada）
欧洲航线	德国汉莎航空公司（Lufthansa） 意大利航空公司（Alitalia） 法国航空公司（Air France） 荷兰皇家航空公司（KLM） 波兰航空（Polish Airlines） 卢森堡国际航空公司（Cargolux Airlines） 奥地利航空公司（Austrian Airlines） 英国航空公司（British Airways）
亚洲航线	中国国际航空公司（Air China） 中国东方航空公司（China Eastern Airlines） 中国西北航空公司（China Northwest Airlines） 中国南方航空公司（China Southwest Airlines） 日本货物航空（Nippon Cargo Airlines） 韩亚航空公司（Asiana Airlines） 新加坡航空公司（Singapore Airlines）

（一）Write and Talk 写脚本，练习电话报价

从前期沟通中，小余对即将电话沟通的杰克先生的商品和需求已经有所了解，为了顺利沟通，他参照资深货代销售员老李的电话报价实录，为自己拟定了如下空运电话报价的中文提纲，并据此写出英文对话。

1. Translation

小余：我是上海前进国际货代公司的小余。我能为您做些什么？
Mr. Yu: _____

杰克：我想要把一批家具从大连托运到德国的卢森堡。能不能给我提供门到门的空运报价？
Jack: _____
_____

小余：当然可以。请问您的家具大概有多重？
Mr. Yu: _____
_____

杰克：大概 115 千克。
Jack: _____

小余：货量？
Mr. Yu: _____
_____

杰克：2 立方米。
Jack: _____

小余：大连报关费 40 美元一票，卫检费是一箱 0.01 美元。货运站处理费是每千克 0.01 美元，从大连到卢森堡的空运费是每千克 3.10 美元，目的地提送货费是 100 美元，目的地清关费是 130 美元一票，目的地关税是 180 美元。这次空运的承运方是中国东方航空公司。
Mr. Yu: _____
_____
_____

杰克：运输需要多少时间。
Jack: _____

小余：每周二从大连飞，运输大约需要 2 天。
Mr. Yu: _____

杰克：我已经接收到这些信息了。等我决定了会再给你打电话的。
Jack: _____

小余：期待您与我们进一步合作。
Mr. Yu: _____

2. Talk

请与同桌练习这部分电话报价。

（二）Act and Practise 扮角色，实施电话报价

与同桌或前后座同学组成两人小组，分别扮演上海前进国际货代公司的销售员小余和他的客户杰克。

（1）"客户杰克"在国际货代、物流公司网站查询空运航线信息，搜索中国各航线城市到各个国际城市的航线信息；设定托运客户询价的信息；设计空运电话询价的语句（表3-1-1）。

表3-1-1 空运电话询价信息设计表

货物名称	
启运地	
目的地	
所用集装箱规格	
所用集装箱数量	
空运电话询价语句摘要	

（2）"销售员小余"在国际货代、物流公司网站查询空运航线信息，搜索中国各航线城市到各个国际城市的航线信息；根据实际航线的空运费用设定国际货代企业报价的信息；设计空运电话报价的语句（表3-1-2）。

表 3-1-2　空运电话报价信息设计表

空运费	
空运费包含项目	
运输时间	
运输频率	
承运方	
报价有效期	
空运电话报价语句摘要	

（3）"客户杰克"与"销售员小余"在电话信息设计表的辅助下，开展对话交流，进行空运电话报价。

（4）对话后，"客户杰克"与"销售员小余"分别用不同颜色的笔对电话信息设计表进行修改。

（5）交换角色，再次完成（1）～（4），充分实践空运电话报价。

【知识检测】

"空运电话报价"这一任务的评价采用自测形式，请学生在实施任务后对于应掌握的词汇或句型进行回顾，完成 Self-check，对于已掌握的，在它前面的括号中打"√"，完成表 3-1-3 的填写。

模块三 空 运

表 3-1-3　空运电话报价知识自测表

Self-check			
I learned:			
(　) GCR	(　) CCR	(　) SCR	(　) customs clearance fee
(　) UCR	(　) ATC	(　) ABF	(　) FSC
(　) SCC	(　) D/O fee	(　) waiting charge	(　) container loading charge
(　) Hello, this is … calling/speaking. What can I help you?			
(　) How many containers are used and what size?			
(　) This air freight rate is … , including …			
(　) The … charge is …			
(　) Please let me know the frequency and the transit time.			
(　) Hold on, please. Let me check.			
(　) I've got it. Thank you, and I'll call you when I've made my decision.			
(　) I'm looking forward to your early reply.			
I can:			
(　) make air quotation by telephone.			

Task Two　Air Email Quotation
任务二　空运邮件报价

【任务导入】

小余是上海前进国际货代公司的实习销售人员，最近准备通过邮件向新客户杰瑞先生进行空运运费的报价。因为是第一次用邮件向新客户进行报价，小余害怕不能很好地完成任务。

请帮助小余一起完成空运邮件报价吧！

【任务实施】

一、巩固空运报价词汇

请先进入知识学苑（3-1-4）开展任务实施前的学习，复习巩固空运报价相关词汇。

知识学苑（3-1-4）——词汇巩固

1. Door to Door / Port——门到门 / 港
2. T/T = Transit Time——运输时间
3. Carrier——承运人
4. Air rate——空运费
5. Air quote for …——……空运报价
6. Handling and accessorial charges——货物处理及其他费用
7. air quotation——空运报价

Read and Match 读词汇，匹配中文

如图 3-1-2 所示，请将空运报价英文表述与中文表述进行正确连线。

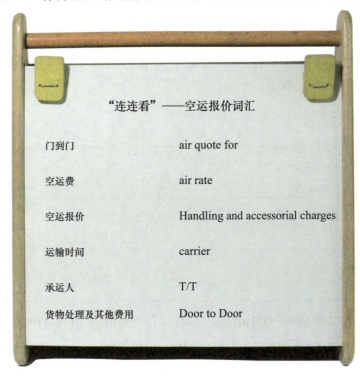

图 3-1-2　常见空运报价词汇中英文配对

二、明确 E-mail 书写格式

请先进入知识学苑（3-1-5）开展任务实施前的学习，掌握电子邮件的写作格式。

模块三 空 运

> **知识学苑（3-1-5）——电子邮件模板**
>
> From: Graford@163.com
> To: Mike@yahoo.com
> Subject: Air quote for Door to Port
> Dear Mr. Lee,
> 　　With great thanks for your enquiry of …(DATE), we now give you our air quotations for Door to Port shipment from… to….
> 　　Air rate: …
> 　　Carrier: …
> 　　T/T: …
> Handling and accessorial charges:
> 　　Airline fuel Surcharge USD …
> 　　THC/CFS USD …
> 　　Customs inspection fee …
> 　　Customs clearance: USD …
> 　　We are looking forward to your confirmation.
> Yours sincerely,
> Kate Weber

（一）Read and Translate 读邮件，翻译邮件报价

勤快的小余跟随在师傅老李左右，将老李与客户往来的空运邮件报价整理出来，并利用空余时间将英文翻译为中文。

From: Karen Lee

译文：_____

To: Anna Jensen

译文：_____

Re: Air quote for Door to Port

译文：_____

Dear Mrs.Jensen,

译文：_____

With great thanks for your enquiry of July 27, we now give you our air quotations for Door to Port shipment from China to Rotterdam.

译文：_____
_____

Air rate: For +100K　　　　USD 3.25/kg
　　　　　For +300K.　　　　USD 3.00/kg

               For +500K.   USD 2.6/kg
               For +1,000K.   USD 2.30/kg

译文：_____

_____

_____

Carrier: CV.

译文：_____

T/T: one day

译文：_____

Handling and accessorial charges:

译文：_____

Airline fuel Surcharge USD 0.10/kg

THC/CFS USD 0.10/kg Min 20 per shipment

Quarantine Inspection Fee: USD 0.20/carton

Customs Clearance: USD USD 40 per shipment

译文：_____

_____

_____

_____

We are looking forward to your confirmation.

译文：_____

（二）Remember and Complete 忆句型，补全邮件报价

为了巩固学习成果，小余反复研究老李的邮件报价实录，努力记忆空运邮件报价的典型句型，并在以下横线上填写缺失的部分词汇。

From: Karen Lee@163.com

To: Mike@yahoo.com

Subject: _____ for Door to Port

Dear Mr. Lee,

With great thanks for your _____ of _____, we now give you our _____ for Door to Port shipment from China to Rotterdam

          _____: For +100K   USD 3.25/kg
                      For +300K.   USD 3.00/kg

模块三 空 运

        For +500K.   USD 2.6/kg

        For +1,000K.   USD 2.30/kg

_____: CV

_____: one day

Handling and_____:

Airline fuel Surcharge USD 0.10/kg

THC/CFS USD 0.10/kg Min 20 per shipment

Quarantine_____fee: USD 0.20/carton

Customs_____: USD 40 per shipment

We are looking forward to your_____.

Yours_____,
Kate Weber

三、实施空运邮件报价任务

（一）Write and Talk 写脚本，练习邮件报价

从前期沟通中，杰瑞先生通过邮件向小余进行了空运询价，小余仔细阅读后，参照资深货代销售员老李的邮件报价实录，拟定了如下空运邮件报价的中文提纲，并据此写出英文邮件。

1. Read and Write 阅读邮件，回复邮件

> From: Jerry Jensen
> To: Xiao Yu
> Date: July 12,2020
> Subject: Air quote for Door to Port
>
> Dear Mr. Yu,
>   I need air quotation for all weight breaks going from Shanghai to London. These quotes are all Door to Port. Do not forget all handling and accessorial charges. If you have any questions, please do not hesitate to let me know.
>   Thanks so much for your help.
>
> Yours sincerely,
> Jerry Jensen

发件人：小余
From：_____
收件人：杰瑞
To：_____
主题：上海到伦敦门到港空运报价
Subject：_____

杰瑞先生，

感谢贵公司于 7 月 12 日的询价，现将从上海到伦敦门到港的空运报价如下：

空运费： 100K 以上　　　　3.25 美元 / 千克
　　　　 300K 以上　　　　3.00 美元 / 千克
　　　　 500K 以上　　　　2.60 美元 / 千克
　　　　 1 000K 以上　　　2.30 美元 / 千克

承运人：中国东航

运输时间：2 天

货物处理及其他费用：

航空燃油费附加费：0.10 美元 / 千克
码头 / 货运站收费：0.10 美元 / 千克
检疫费：0.20 美元 / 千克
清关费：40 美元 / 票

我们期待贵公司的确认

此致
敬礼
小余

2. Write

请将完整的英文回复邮件整理如下：

（二）Act and Practise 扮角色，实施邮件报价

与同桌或前后座同学组成两人小组，分别扮演上海国际货代公司的销售员小余和他的客户杰瑞。

（1）"客户杰瑞"在国际货代、物流公司网站查询空运航线信息，搜索中国各航线城市到国际主要城市的航线信息；设定托运客户询价的信息；设计空运邮件询价的语句，完成表3-1-4。

表 3-1-4　海运邮件询价信息设计表

货物名称	
启运地	
目的地	
空运询价邮件	

（2）"销售员小余"在国际货代、物流公司网站查询空运航线信息，搜索中国各航线城市到国际主要城市的航线信息；设定托运客户报价的信息；设计空运报价的邮件，完成表 3-1-5。

表 3-1-5　海运邮件报价信息设计表

空运费	
空运费包含项目	
运输时间	
运输频率	
承运人	
空运报价邮件	

（3）"客户杰瑞"与"销售员小余"在邮件报价信息设计表的辅助下，开展邮件交流，进行空运邮件报价。

（4）沟通后，"客户杰瑞"与"销售员小余"分别用不同颜色的笔对邮件报价信息设计表进行修改。

【知识检测】

"空运邮件报价"这一任务的评价采用自测形式，请学生在实施任务后对于应掌握的词汇或句型进行回顾，完成 Self-check，对于已掌握的，在它前面的括号中打"√"，完成表 3-1-6 的填写。

表 3-1-6　空运邮件报价知识自测表

Self-check				
I learned:				
（　）carrier	（　）T/T		（　）quarantine inspection	（　）customs clearance fee
（　）air rate	（　）accessorial charges		（　）handling charges	（　）air quotation
（　）I need air quotation for …				
（　）These quotes are all …				
（　）with great thanks for your enquiry of …, we now give our air quotations for …				
（　）The … charge is …				
（　）We are all looking forward to your confirmation.				
I can:				
（　）make air quotation by e-mails.				

项目二
空运操作
Project Two Air Freight Operation

【学习目标】

1. 能阅读空运信函，并熟悉空运主要港口、航线以及公司。
2. 能读懂并填制英文空运票据，并熟悉危险品的特殊空运操作流程。
3. 在学习空运操作的过程中，培养爱岗敬业的职业精神。

Task One Major Ports, Routes and Companies of Air Freight

任务一 认识空运主要港口、航线及公司

【任务导入】

小余跟着师傅学习空运业务，不过小余发现老李和客户谈的许多空运港口和航线，与之前学习过的海运港口和航线完全不同。老李告诉小余不要着急，与学习海运业务一样，要熟悉空运主要的港口、航线和船公司，这可以帮助货代员快速有效地与客户沟通协调，更是合格的空运货代员的必由之路。

接下来就请与小余一起认识一下空运的主要港口、航线和航空运输公司吧！

【任务实施】

一、认识空运主要航线和港口

请先进入知识学苑（3-2-1）开展任务实施前的学习，认识空运主要航线和港口。

知识学苑（3-2-1）——空运主要航线和港口

（一）空运主要航线及航线主要航空港

1. 北大西洋航空线（North Atlantic air route）

该航线的主要航空港有巴黎（Paris）、伦敦（London）、法兰克福（Frankfurt）、纽约（New York）、芝加哥（Chicago）、蒙特利亚（Monteria）等。

2. 西欧—中东—远东航空线（Western Europe-Middle East-Far East Air Line）

该航线的主要航空港有香港（Hong Kong）、北京（Beijing）、东京（Tokyo）、雅典（Athens）、开罗（Cairo）、德黑兰（Tehran）、卡拉奇（Karachi）、新德里（New Delhi）、曼谷（Bangkok）、新加坡（Singapore）等。

3. 北太平洋航空线（North Pacific air route）

该航线的主要航空港有北京（Beijing）、香港（Hong Kong）、东京（Tokyo）、温哥华（Vancouver）、西雅图（Seattle）、旧金山（San Francisco）、洛杉矶（Los Angeles）等。火奴鲁鲁（Honolulu）是该航线的主要中继加油站。

4. 其他重要航线

（1）北美—南美航线（North America-South America Route）。
（2）西欧—南美航线（Route between Western Europe and South America）。
（3）西欧—非洲航线（West Europe-Africa Route）。
（4）西欧—东南亚航线（Western Europe-Southeast Asia Route）。
（5）远东—澳新航线（Far East-Australia New Route）。
（6）北美—澳新航线（North America-Australia New Route）。

（二）各大洲主要航空港

1. 北美洲航空港（North American airports）：华盛顿（Washington）、纽约（New York）、芝加哥（Chicago）、蒙特利尔（Montreal）、亚特兰大（Atlanta）、洛杉矶（Los Angeles）、旧金山（San Francisco）、西雅图（Seattle）等（etc.）。

2. 欧洲航空港（European airports）：伦敦（London）、巴黎（Paris）、法兰克福（Frankfurt）、苏黎世（Zurich）、罗马（Rome）、维也纳（Vienna）、柏林（Berlin）、哥本哈根（Copenhagen）、华沙（Warsaw）、莫斯科（Moscow）、布加勒斯特（Bucharest）、雅典（Athens）等（etc.）。

3. 非洲航空港（African airports）：开罗（Cairo）、喀土穆（Khartoum）、内罗毕（Nairobi）、约翰内斯堡（Johannesburg）、布拉柴维尔（Brazzaville）、拉各斯（Lagos）、达喀尔（Dakar）、阿尔及尔（Algiers）等（etc.）。

4. 亚洲航空港（Asian airports）：北京（Beijing）、上海（Shanghai）、东京（Tokyo）、香港（Hong Kong）、马尼拉（Manila）、曼谷（Bangkok）、仰光（Yangon）、加尔各答（Kolkata）、孟买（Mumbai）、卡拉奇（Karachi）、贝鲁特（Beirut）等（etc.）。

5. 拉美航空港（Latin American airports）：墨西哥城（Mexico City）、加拉加斯（Caracas）、里约热内卢（Rio DE Janeiro）、布宜诺斯艾利斯（Buenos Aires）、圣地亚哥（Santiago）、利马（Lima）等（etc.）。

6. 大洋洲及太平洋岛屿航空港（Oceania and Pacific Island Airports）：悉尼（Sydney）、奥克兰（Auckland）、楠迪（Nandi）、火奴鲁鲁（Honolulu）等（etc.）。

（一）Read and Choose 读航线，选择港口名称

在"知识学苑"中学习了空运主要航线和港口之后，小余认识了不少进出口空运的

关键航线及航线主要航空港。他尝试将航线及航线主要航空港进行正确匹配。

A. 属于北大西洋航空线（North Atlantic air route）的港口有：	B. 属于西欧—中东—远东航空线（Western Europe – Middle East – Far East Air Line）的港口有：	C. 属于北太平洋航空线（North Pacific air route）的港口有：
A. Hong Kong　　B. Beijing　　C. Tokyo　　D. Washington　　E. New York F. Chicago　　　G. Athens　　　H. Cairo　　　I. Los Angeles J. Vancouver　　K. San Francisco　L. Seattle			

（二）Read and Mark：读英文，匹配区域名称

在熟悉了空运主要航线之后，小余很想检验自己的学习成果。他需要熟读这些港口的英文名称，并标记出他们所在的大洲（区域）名称。

(a) Mexico City（　　）

(b) Caracas（　　）

(c) Tokyo（　　）

(d) Hong Kong（　　）

(e) Dakar（　　）

(f) Algiers（　　）

(g) Karachi（　　）

(h) Washington（　　）

(i) New York（　　）

(j) London（　　）

(k) Paris（　　）

(l) Sydney（　　）

(m) Auckland（　　）

(n) Kolkata（　　）

二、认识中外主要航空公司

请先进入知识学苑（3-2-2）和（3-2-3）开展任务实施前的准备，认识中国及世界主要航空公司。

	知识学苑（3-2-2）——世界主要航空公司			
序号	中文名	英文名（缩写代码）	公司图标	总部机场
1	英国航空公司	BRITISH AIRWAYS（BA）	BRITISH AIRWAYS	伦敦希斯罗机场
2	法国航空公司	AIR FRANCE（AF）	AIR FRANCE	戴高乐机场
3	德国汉莎航空公司	LUFTHANSA（LH）	Lufthansa	法兰克福机场
4	新加坡航空公司	SINGAPORE AIRLINES（SQ）	SINGAPORE AIRLINES	新加坡樟宜国际机场
5	美国联合航空公司	UNITED AIRLINES（UA）	UNITED	芝加哥奥黑国际机场
6	日本航空公司	JAPAN AIRLINES（JL）	JAL	东京成田国际机场
7	荷兰皇家航空	ROYAL DUTCH AIRLINES（KL）	KLM	阿姆斯特丹史基浦国际机场
8	美国航空公司	AMERICAN AIRLINES（AA）	AA American Airlines	得克萨斯沃斯堡机场
9	澳洲航空公司	QANTAS AIRLINES（QF）	QANTAS THE SPIRIT OF AUSTRALIA	悉尼金斯福德国际机场

知识学苑（3-2-3）——我国主要航空公司			
序号	公司名称	缩写	图标
1	中国国际航空公司	CA	AIR CHINA 中国国际航空公司
2	中国南方航空公司	CZ	中国南方航空 CHINA SOUTHERN AIRLINES
3	中国东方航空公司	MU	中国东方航空 CHINA EASTERN
4	山东航空公司	SC	山东航空公司 SHANDONG AIRLINES
5	厦门航空公司	MF	厦门航空 XIAMENAIR
6	海南航空公司	HU	海南航空 Hainan Airlines
7	四川航空公司	3U	四川航空 SICHUAN AIRLINES
8	深圳航空公司	ZH	深圳航空 Shenzhen Airlines

（一）Choose and Match 做选择，完成连线匹配

小余为了更好、更快地熟悉航空公司名称及其缩写代码，将以上航空公司的名称和代码进行混合，如图 3-2-1 所示，帮小余快速地连线完成匹配吧。

模块三 空 运

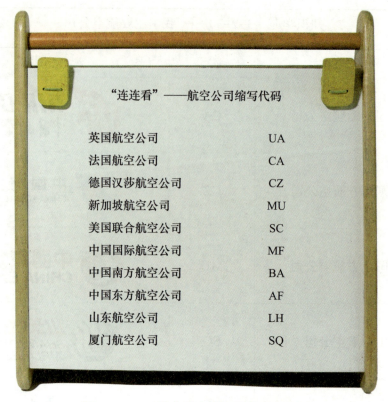

图 3-2-1　航空公司缩写代码配对

（二）Read and Judge 读短文，完成判断

1. Read

Air transport is a method of transport using aircraft, helicopters and other aircraft to transport people, goods and mails, generally applicable to valuables, fresh goods, precision instruments goods. Air freight forwarders mainly focus the use of routes, airports, aircraft and assembly equipment.

Air freight forwarders usually handle the business of soliciting, receiving, customs declaration, booking space, picking up goods at the destination airport and delivering the goods to the consignee. Usually, air freight forwarders act as agents for both shippers and airlines. It may accept the cargo on behalf of the airline and issue an air waybill. When the cargo is lost or damaged within the scope of the airline's liability, it may claim compensation from the airline on behalf of the cargo owner.

【参考译文】

航空运输是使用飞机、直升机及其他航空器运送人员、货物、邮件的一种运输方式，一般适用于贵重物品、鲜活货物、精密仪器商品。空运货代主要把握好航线、航空港、航空器以及集装设备的利用。

空运货代通常办理揽货、接货、报关、订舱，及在目的地机场提货和将货物交付给收货人等方面的业务，简称空代。通常空代既是货主的代理又是航空公司的代理。它可代表航空公司接受货主的货物并出具航空分运单，当货物在航空公司责任范围内丢失或损坏时，他又可代表货主向航空公司索赔。

2. Judge

☐ (1) Air freight forwarders mainly focus the use of routes, airports, aircraft and assembly equipment.

☐ (2) Air freight forwarders usually handle the business of soliciting, receiving, customs declaration, booking space, picking up goods at the destination airport and delivering the goods to the consignee.

☐ (3) Usually, shippers act as agents for both air freight forwarders and airlines.

☐ (4) When the cargo is lost or damaged within the scope of the airline's liability, it can't claim compensation from the airline on behalf of the cargo owner.

【知识检测】

"认识空运主要港口、航线和公司"这一任务的评价采用自测形式，请学生在实施任务后对于应掌握的词汇进行回顾，完成 Self-check，对于已掌握的，在它前面的括号中打"√"，填写表 3-2-1。

表 3-2-1　认识空运主要港口、航线和公司自测表

Self-check			
I learned:			
(　) BA	(　) AF	(　) LH	(　) SQ
(　) UA	(　) JL	(　) KL	(　) AA
(　) NW	(　) QI	(　) CA	(　) CZ
(　) MU	(　) SC	(　) MF	(　) HU
(　) 3U	(　) ZH		
(　) North Atlantic air route			
(　) Western Europe-Middle East-Far East Air Line			
(　) North Pacific air route			
I can:			
(　) recognize the major ports, routes and companies of Air Freight.			

模块三 空 运

Task Two　Reading Air Mails
任务二　阅读空运信函

【任务导入】

在认识了空运主要港口、航线及公司后，小余发现自己还是看不懂师傅用邮件跟美国客户沟通的内容。师傅说：不想做空运货代的"门外汉"，就必须能读懂行业沟通的法宝"空运信函"，而空运信函里遍布标准的操作流程和专用术语。

请与小余一起阅读空运信函吧！

【任务实施】

一、明确进出口空运关键业务

请先进入知识学苑（3-2-4）开展任务实施前的学习，明确进出口空运关键业务。

知识学苑（3-2-4）——进出口空运业务与相关单证

进出口空运货代操作相关的关键业务信息（含各类信函）是空运货物从入境到提取再到转运各个环节涉及的内容。空运信函的主要沟通内容包括以下组成部分：

（一）进口空运关键业务
（1）接单接货（receiving orders and receiving goods）。
（2）货物进仓（warehousing）。
（3）单据录入（documents）。
（4）发到货通知（send the arrival notice）。
（5）制作报关单（make out customs declaration form）。
（6）进口商品检验检疫（commodity inspection）。
（7）进口报关（import customs clearance）。
（8）送货或转运（delivery or transshipment）。

（二）进口空运业务基本单证
（1）航空运单（air waybill）。
（2）货物报关单（declaration of goods）。
（3）货物发票（invoice）。
（4）货物装箱单（packing list）。
（5）商检证明（inspection certificate）。
（6）进口许可证（import license）。

114

（三）出口空运业务关键业务

（1）销售（sales）。
（2）订舱（booking）。
（3）接单接货（receive orders and goods）。
（4）制单（make documents）。
（5）出口商品检验检疫（inspection）。
（6）出口报关（export declaration）。
（7）出口核销（export verification）。
（8）发运货物（transport）。
（9）交接货物（handover of good）。
（10）费用结算（charge settlement）。

（四）出口空运业务基本单证

（1）中华人民共和国海关出口货物报关单（declaration form for export goods issued by the customs of the People's Republic of China）。
（2）国际空运货物委托书（letter of authorization）。
（3）发票与装箱单（invoice and packing list）。
（4）合同副本（copy of the contract）。
（5）航空运单（air waybill）。
（6）商检证明（inspection certificate）。
（7）进口许可证（export license）。

*（五）特殊商品出口业务

（1）包机运输（charter transportation）。
解释：航空公司既是承运人又是代理人
（2）挂衣箱运输（trunk transportation）。
解释：高档服装出口申请挂衣箱服务
（3）私人物品运输（transport of personal belongings）。
解释：来华人员私人大件物品的运输
（4）鲜活易腐物品运输（transport of fresh goods）。
解释：必要时需要提供合格证明和卫生检疫证明
（5）危险品运输（transport of dangerous goods）。
解释：发货人必须提供危险品的化学和物理成分报告，商检机构出具相关危险品证明并根据不同危险品等级在外包装粘贴标志
（6）贵重物品运输（valuables transportation）。
解释：需要发货人声明价值并在包装标记"贵重物品"字样
（7）活体动物运输（live animal transport）。
解释：需要出具动物检疫合格证明并提供动物生活习性资料
（8）尸体和骨灰运输（transport of body and ashes）。
解释：需要开具死亡证明和火化证明等

（一）Read and Match 读词组，匹配业务名称

尝试用连线的方式完成以下三组关键业务和单证类型的中英文配对。

1. 匹配进口空运关键业务

如图 3-2-2 所示，将进口空运关键业务的中英文进行配对。

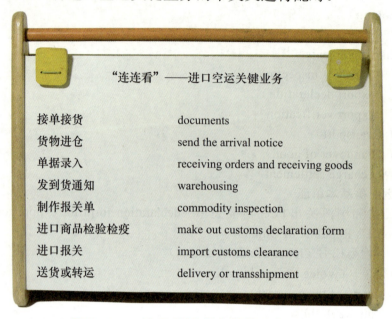

图 3-2-2　进口空运业务关键业务匹配

2. 匹配出口空运关键业务

如图 3-2-3 所示，将出口空运关键业务的中英文进行配对。

图 3-2-3　出口空运业务关键业务匹配

3. 进出口空运单证匹配

如图 3-2-4 所示，将单证与进、出口空运业务进行匹配，属于进口的与左边方框相连，属于出口的与右边方框相连。

图 3-2-4　进出口空运单证匹配

（二）Read and Judge 读短文，辨析空运信函要点

在正式与客人进行函电沟通前，小余还要明确一份标准的空运信函应该包括哪些要点和需要注意之处。

阅读以下短文，完成与空运信函要点相关的判断，在正确的表述前面打"√"，并进行朗读；在错误的表述前面打"×"，并订正该说法。

1. Read

International air freight import and export agent's timeline is strong. There are a lot of terms and abbreviations in letters. This is to coordinate and ensure the delivery of goods. Between the large consignee (shipper) and the transport enterprise, among the various departments of the transportation enterprise, business correspondence has its own standard operating procedures. The main items are: document submission time, waybill making requirements, packing guarantee, airline selection, cargo declaration, cargo distribution, etc.

Air freight operators only need to follow the rules strictly. In particular, the use of abbreviations and terms can improve the efficiency of correspondence. In the letter writing, we should pay special attention to strict and standard language. Be careful to use the special vocabulary in air freight import and export.

【参考译文】

国际空运进出口代理的时效性强、规范性强,最值得一提的是信函中委托双方存在着大量简洁的缩写和函电术语,以此协调并保证货物顺利地出运。大的收货人(发货人)与运输行之间、运输公司各部门之间往来的信函都有标准的操作流程和专用术语,主要的有:文件递交的时间、运单制作要求、装箱保证、航空公司选择、货物报关、配送分拨等。

空运操作人员只需要严格照章办事即可,尤其是使用缩写和术语可以提高函电效率。信函写作中尤其要注意语言的严谨规范。在空运进出口业务中要细心把握遣词用语。

2. Judge

☐ (1) International air freight import and export agent's deadline is strong.

☐ (2) Between the large shipper and consignee, there is a standard operating procedure.

☐ (3) Air mails' items are: document submission time, waybill making requirements, packing guarantee, airline selection, cargo declaration, cargo distribution, etc.

☐ (4) In the letter writing, we should pay special attention to casual language firstly.

二、学习进出口空运信函表达

请先进入知识学苑(3-2-5)开展任务实施前的准备,学习进出口空运信函的常用表达。

知识学苑(3-2-5)——进出口空运信函的常用表达

进出口空运信函有标准的操作流程和专用术语,主要包括文件递交的时间、运单制作要求、装箱保证、航空公司选择、货物报关、配送分拨等内容。常用表达如下。

(一)专心识别基本信息

e.x.1. A/F SHPT FOR C/ ... TO ...(收货人 A 空运至 B 处)

(1)A/F=air freight(空运)。

(2)SHPT=shipment(航次)。

(3)C/=consignee(收货人)。

e.x.2. RE: S/: ……(收货人和发货人基本信息提供)

C/...

(1)RE: = regarding(关于……的内容)。

(2)S/=shipper(发货人)。

(3)C/=consignee(收货人)。

(4)SUBJECT…(邮件的主题是……)。

（二）用心分析货品数据

e.x.1. COMM: A（商品 A）

ORDER NO 693（订单号：693）

28 CTNS/196 KGS/0.672 CBM（28 纸箱，196 公斤，0.672 立方米）

A/F CC FM C/（空运到付收货人）

（1）COMM:= commodity（商品、货品）。

（2）ORDER NO.（订单号）。

（3）CTN=carton（纸箱）。

（4）CBM= cubic meter（立方米）。

（5）CC=charges collect（到付货）。

（6）FM TO =from…to…（从……到……）。

e.x.2 FLIGHT IS ETD A 11/23 VIA B N OUR COST IS USD 3.78/KG（航班预计 11 月 23 日起飞并交货，费用为每公斤 3.78 美元）

（1）ETD= estimated time of delivery（预计交货时间）。

（2）N=and（和）。

（3）USD（美元）。

（三）悉心筹划遣词用句

e.x.1. PLS RELAY IT TO C/AND O/N REPLY IS APPRECIATED（请将其传至收货人并盼望第二天的答复）

（1）PLS=please（请）。

（2）RELAY IT TO（传送至）。

（3）C/=consignee（收货人）。

（4）O/N=overnight（过夜的，第二天）。

（5）REPLY IS APPRECIATED（期待回复）。

e.x.2. PLS SEND PRE-ALERT, DOCS D/N ASAP（请尽快发送预报和借据文件）

（1）PLS=please（请）。

（2）PRE-ALERT（预报）。

（3）DOCS=documents（文件）。

（4）D/N= Debit note（借据）。

（5）ASAP=As soon as possible（越快越好）。

e.x.3. HAWB AND MAWB HV PREPARED（主单和分单都已经准备好了）

（1）HV=have（已经完成）。

（2）HAWB=house airway bill（航空运单分单）。

（3）MAWB=master airway bill（航空运单主单）。

（四）留心对方延伸沟通

e.x.1. FURTHER TO THE MESSAGE SENT TO U, PLS RE-CHECK KGS FOR THIS ORDER ADV ASAP（进一步的消息提供给你方，请再次尽快确认此单的重量通知）

（1）ASAP=As soon as possible（越快越好）。

（2）U=you（你方）。

（3）ADV=advice（通知）。

（4）ASAP=As soon as possible（越快越好）。

（5）PLS=please（请）。

模块三 空 运

e.x.2. HE WAS EXPECTING APPROX 30 KGS. PLS ADV（对方大概期待需要 30 公斤重，请通知一下。

（1）APPROX（大约，大概）。

（2）PLS=please（请）。

（3）ADV=advice（通知）。

（五）细心剖析交换信息

e.x.1. THE ACTUAL GROSS WT IS 97KGS N VOLUME WT IS 158.7 KG AND MEASMT IS 0.952 CBM. S/ FAIL TO CLEAR CUSTOMS（实际毛重是 97 公斤，体积重量计算为 158.7 公斤，尺码计算重量为 0.952 立方米。发货人无法正常清关。）

（1）GROSS WT（毛重）。

（2）VOLUME WT（体积重量）。

（3）MEASMT（尺码、尺寸）。

（4）S/（发货人）。

e.x.2. PREPARING FOR CORRECT DOC AND WL SEND TO US TMRW TO CLEAR CUSTOMS AGN.（准备好正确的文件发送给我方，明天将再次办理报关）

（1）DOC=document（文件）。

（2）US（我方）。

（3）TMRW=tomorrow（明天）。

（4）AGN=again（再次）。

（5）WL=will（将会）。

（一）Write and Match 做重复匹配训练

在"知识学苑"中学习了进出口空运信函的常用表达后，小余掌握了不少空运信函涉及的术语缩写，他尝试根据对照中文和英文翻译，将缩写写下来。

（_____）=air freight（空运）

（_____）=shipment（航次）

（_____）=consignee（收货人）

（_____）=shipper（发货人）

（_____）= regarding（关于……的内容）

（_____）=commodity（商品、货品）

（_____）=carton（纸箱）

（_____）=cubic meter（立方米）

（_____）=charges collect（到付货）

（_____）=from…to…（从……到……）

（_____）=estimated time of delivery（预计交货时间）

（_____）=and（和）

（_____）=please（请）

（_____）=your（你方的）

（　　　　　　　）=overnight（过夜的，第二天）
（　　　　　　　）=documents（文件）
（　　　　　　　）= Debit note(借据)
（　　　　　　　）=As soon as possible（越快越好）
（　　　　　　　）=you（你方）
（　　　　　　　）=advice（通知）
（　　　　　　　）=have（已经完成）
（　　　　　　　）=tomorrow（明天）
（　　　　　　　）=again（再次）
（　　　　　　　）=will（将会）
（　　　　　　　）=flight（航班）
（　　　　　　　）=house airway bill（航空运单分单）
（　　　　　　　）=master airway bill（航空运单主单）

（二）Read and Translate 读信函，翻译信函主要内容

在学习了进出口空运信函涉及的缩写后，小余终于有了信心，他下定决心：咬定青山不放松，一定要啃下这块硬骨头。于是小余在师傅的帮助下，对海运信函逐词逐句进行翻译，尤其是将各种信函缩写部分进行了勾画和标注。功夫不负有心人，小余已经能够顺利地阅读师傅发给美国客户的信函啦！

From: Emma (Shanghai) To: Carrie (USA)
Subject: A/F SHPT FOR C/××× TO ×××
DEAR CARRIE RE: S/: NEW SUCCESS HOLDINGS LIMITED C/:ABC COMM: WOODEN DISPLAY RACI ORDER NO 693 28 CTNS/196 KGS/0.672 CBM A/F CC FM C/ FM ××× TO ××× AS THE CARGO WILL ARRIVE IN THE WAREHOUSE ON 11/22 MORNING, THE FIRST DIRECT FLIGHT IS ETD SHA 11/23 VIA MU N OUR COST IS USD 3.78/KG PLS RELAY IT TO C/AND UR O/N REPLY IS APPRECIATED

1. Circle

请将此信函中的进出口空运术语缩写圈出来，并摘录在下方横线上，注明其中文名称。

_____

_____

_____

_____

2. Translate

请尝试翻译以下信函内容。

(1) "RE: S/: NEW SUCCESS HOLDINGS LIMITED
  C/: ABC"

译文：_____

_____

_____

(2) "COMM: WOODEN DISPLAY RACI
  ORDER NO 693
  28 CTNS/196 KGS/0.672 CBM
  A/F CC FM C/"

译文：_____

_____

_____

_____

（3）"AS THE CARGO WILL ARRIVE IN THE WAREHOUSE ON 11/22 MORNING, THE FIRST DIRECT FLIGHT IS ETD SHA 11/23 VIA MU N OUR COST IS USD 3.78/KG"

译文：_____

_____

_____

_____

（三）Fill and comprehend 补信函，理解缩写词汇搭配

师傅将美国客户回复给自己的空运信函从收件箱里找了出来，小余喜出望外。师傅故意卖了个关子，将信函里的术语缩写全部删除，并在旁边备注了中文提示。小余能顺利地将这些术语补全吗？下面就由你跟小余一起完成吧。

1. Fill

From: Carrie (USA)　　　　To: Emma(Shanghai)
OK TO SHIP VIA＿＿＿（1）＿＿＿（空运）TO ×××＿＿＿（2）＿＿＿（请）SEND PRE-ALERT, ＿＿＿（3）＿＿＿（文件）D/N＿＿＿（4）＿＿＿（尽可能快的）
From: Carrie (USA)　　To: Emma (Shanghai)
FURTHER TO THE MESSAGE SENT TO U, PLS RE-CHECK＿＿＿（5）＿＿＿（重量）FOR THIS ORDER＿＿＿（6）＿＿＿（传达，传递）＿＿＿（7）＿＿＿（尽可能快的）＿＿＿（8）＿＿＿（发货人）SAYS 196 KGS IS FINE HE STILL WANTS TO PROCEED WITH AIR FREIGHT TO ××× HE WAS EXPECTING APPROX 30 KGS. PLS＿＿＿（9）＿＿＿（传达，传递）

2. Choose

From: Emma　　　　To: Carrie
HV（□已经/□尚未）ASKED S/（□发货人/□收货人）TO RECHECK KGS BUT GW（□毛重/□净重人）IS STILL 196 KGS
From: Emma　　　　To: Carrie
AFTER BEING WEIGHED AT OUR HANDLING WAREHOUSE,THE ACTUAL GROSS WT IS 97 KGS N（□和/□或）VOLUME WT（□重量/□体积）IS 158.7 KG AND MEASMT（□尺寸/□距离） IS 0.952 CBM. S/ FAIL TO CLEAR CUSTOMS AS ALL DOCUMENT FOR CUSTOMS CLEARANCE OFFERED BY S/（□发货人/□收货人）SHOWS 196 KG. NOW S/（□发货人/□收货人）PREPARING FOR CORRECT DOC AND WILL SEND TO US TMRW（□今天/□明天人）TO CLEAR CUSTOMSAGN. SO THE SHPT CANT CATCH 11/23S FLIGHT AND WL BE DELAYED TO 11/24S FLT RE UR REQUEST NOT TO PUT ACTUAL WEIGHT BUT ONLY PUT CHARGEABLE WEIGHT ON HAWB（□主航空运单/□分航空运单）AND MAWB（□主航空运单/□分航空运单） FOR CHESTA A/F SHPT, PLS NOTE ACTUAL GROSS WEIGHT MUST BE SHOWN ACCORDING TO AIRLINES REGULATION

（四）Read and Translate 阅读信函，对关键内容进行翻译

下面是美国客户进一步沟通的信函，师傅让小余进行详细翻译，请帮助小余翻译下面的内容。

1. Read

IF GROSS WEIGHT SHOWS THE SAME AS CW WHICH IS 158.7 KGS, S/CANT CLEAR CUSTOMS.AS ALL DOC FOR CUSTOMS CLEARANCE MUST SHOW 97 KGS.SO MAWB MUST SHOW 97 KG AS GW AND 158.7 KG AS CW AND WE WILL HV HAWB TO READ.

2. Translate

（1）S/CANT CLEAR CUSTOMS.AS ALL DOC FOR CUSTOMS CLEARANCE

模块三 空 运

MUST SHOW 97 KGS.

译文：_____

_____

（2）MAWB MUST SHOW 97 KG AS GW AND 158.7 KG AS CW AND WE WILL HV HAWB TO READ.

译文：_____

_____

【知识检测】

"阅读空运信函"这一任务的评价采用自测形式，请学生在实施任务后对于应掌握的词汇或句型进行回顾，完成Self-check，对于已掌握的，在它前面的括号中打"√"，完成表3-2-2的填写。

表3-2-2 阅读空运信函知识自测表

Self-check			
I learned:			
（　）A/F	（　）SHPT	（　）C/	（　）S/
（　）RE	（　）COMM	（　）CTN	（　）CBM
（　）CC	（　）FM TO	（　）ETD	（　）N
（　）PLS	（　）UR	（　）O/N	（　）DOCS
（　）D/N	（　）ASAP	（　）U	（　）ADV
（　）HV	（　）TMRW	（　）AGN	（　）FLT
（　）HAWB	（　）MAWB		
（　）Import air transport business key business			
（　）Basic documents for import air freight service			
（　）Export air transport business key business			
（　）Basic documents for import air freight service			
（　）Special goods export business			
I can:			
（　）read the air mails.			

Module Four After-sale Service
模块四 售后服务

项目一 客户异议
Project One Customer Complaint

【学习目标】

1. 能与投诉客户进行有效沟通。
2. 能运用通信工具对客户异议进行回复和处理。
3. 在处理客户异议的过程中，培养谦和有礼的服务态度。

Task One Understanding Common Customer Complaint
任务一 认识常见客户异议

【任务导入】

莎莎是上海前进国际货代公司客服部的一名实习生，王琳是莎莎的师父。王琳手头有一些客户投诉案件，希望莎莎在正式上岗前先进行案件学习。

【任务实施】

一、了解常见客户异议类型

请先进入知识学苑（4-1-1）开展任务实施前的准备，学习常见的客户异议类型。

> 知识学苑（4-1-1）——常见的客户异议类型
>
> 客户异议（Customer Complaint）是指在服务过程中，客户对销售人员或产品提出质疑，或无法达成共识的情况。在货代行业中，关于售后服务的投诉一般包括以下几种：
> （1）Loss of goods ——货物损失。
> （2）Goods arrival delay ——货物到达延迟。
> （3）Return and exchange ——退换货。
> （4）Commodity maintenance ——商品维修。

（一）Read and Choose 读句子，选择异议类型

在"知识学苑"中学习了售后服务的常见客户异议类型后，莎莎从客户投诉案件中发现大部分的异议诉求都可以被归类到相关类型当中，她打算将客户异议分别归类到4种类型中。

读以下英文内容判断属于哪种客户异议类型，并在（   ）中填写异议类型所对应的序号。

（1）Oh, no. I can't find my goods. Did you send it?　　　　　　　　　　（   ）

（2）The grapes I have received are not enough 20 kg per crate.　　　　（   ）

（3）The central air conditioner ordered by our company before nine months are broken. What should we do? It's still under warranty.　　　　　　　　　　　　（   ）

（4）What's the matter with you? I ordered the thick blue cloth, not green one.　（   ）

① Loss of goods　　　　　　　　② Goods arrival delay
③ Return and exchange　　　　　④ Commodity maintenance

（二）Translate and Match 翻译短语，匹配同义表达

在案例学习的过程中，莎莎发现由于客户的习惯不同，相同的客户异议类型可以用不同的英文短语来表达。让我们跟莎莎一起来理解客户的意思，尝试同义替换吧。

1. Translate 英译中

① Item repair　　　　　　　　　　　　中文：_____
② the goods exchange and return　　　中文：_____
③ Goods missing　　　　　　　　　　　中文：_____
④ Not arriving on time　　　　　　　　中文：_____

2. Match 同义替换

① Loss of goods　　　　　　　　　　　英文替换：_____
② Goods arrival delay　　　　　　　　英文替换：_____
③ Return and exchange　　　　　　　　英文替换：_____
④ Commodity maintenance　　　　　　　英文替换：_____

二、明确客户异议常用句型

请先进入知识学苑（4-1-2）开展任务实施前的准备，学习客户提出异议的常用句型。

知识学苑（4-1-2）——客户异议常用句型

接到关于售后方面的客户投诉电话后，既要保持专业态度，保持礼貌和微笑，也要精准了解客户的投诉诉求，及时有效地做好记录，便于跟进处理。

（一）客户异议常用句型

1. I hope you can give me a proper explanation.
   我希望你能给我一个合理的解释。
2. You should have paid for my loss.
   你应该赔偿我的损失。
3. I want to make complaints about your delivery/ marketing.
   我要投诉你们的配送部门/市场部门。
4. The goods I ordered have not been received. What's wrong with it?
   我订购的货物还没有收到，怎么回事？
5. This is not the color I want. I want to exchange it.
   这不是我想要的颜色。我要换一下。

（二）客服应答常用句型

1. OK. Hold on, please. Let me check the goods' information.
   好的，请稍等，我查一下货物信息。
2. I have to make an apology for your loss at first.
   首先，我对您的损失表示抱歉。
3. Could you tell me the details about that?
   您能告诉我具体的情况吗？
4. I'm so sorry to hear it, and I need several minutes to ask for information.
   很抱歉听到这个消息，我需要几分钟了解一下情况。
5. This is a beautiful mistake. We will make up for your loss as soon as possible.
   这是一个美丽的错误。我们会尽快弥补您的损失。

（一）Remember and Complete 忆句型，补全对话

让我们跟莎莎一起回顾一下新学的客户投诉常用句型，并将下列对话补全。

（1）C: It's unbelievable. I hope you can＿＿＿＿＿me a＿＿＿＿＿explanation.

　　R: I have to make an＿＿＿＿＿for your loss＿＿＿＿＿ ＿＿＿＿＿. Due to the weather, it was delayed for a few days.

（2）C: You should have＿＿＿＿＿ ＿＿＿＿＿my loss.

　　R: This is a＿＿＿＿＿mistake. We will＿＿＿＿＿up for your loss as soon as＿＿＿＿＿.

（3）C: I want to make＿＿＿＿＿about your＿＿＿＿＿.

R: What is the problem? I need_____minutes to ask for_____.

（4）C: The goods I_____have not been received. What's_____with it?

R: Hold on, _____. Let me_____the goods' information.

（5）C: This is not the color I_____. I want to_____it.

R: I'm so sorry. Could you_____me the_____about that?

（二）Read and Translate 朗读对话，并翻译

通过句型学习，莎莎变得更自信了。她找来小伙伴小方一起来练习对话，并将对话翻译成中文。

(Fang: a customer

Sasha: a customer service representative)

Fang: Hello，are you Shanghai Qianjin International Forwarder Co., Ltd. ?

译文：_____

Sasha: Yes，this is customer service representative Sasha. What can I do for you?

译文：_____

Fang: I'm a customer of your company. Two weeks ago, I ordered a batch of silk in your company. It should have arrived the day before yesterday, but I haven't received it yet now. What's wrong with it?

译文：_____
_____

Sasha: Could you tell me some details about your name and your order number?

译文：_____

Fang: Fine. Mr. Fang, and my order number is 377429608.

译文：_____

Sasha: OK. Hold on, please. Let me check the goods' information.

译文：_____

Sasha: Mr. Fang, the logistics shows that your goods are being cleared. Please wait patiently.

译文：_____

Fang: What? I hope you can give me a proper explanation.

译文：_____

Sasha: I'm so sorry about that. Due to the weather, it was delayed for a few days. Don't worry, it will arrive soon.

译文：_____

模块四　售后服务

Fang: All right, I hope so.
译文：_____

（三）Phrase and Write 学习短语，并造句

莎莎翻看资料时看到一个案例：新丰实业的王女士委托上海前进国际货代公司进口一批智利车厘子，到货后发现由于包装不当造成了30%的货物损失。王女士非常生气，打来电话投诉。请根据该情境，使用以下英文短语进行造句。

（1）be paid for/paid for　　　　　　　　　含义：_____
造句：_____

（2）make complaints/ make a complaint　　　含义：_____
造句：_____

（3）check sth. information/ ask for information　含义：_____
造句：_____

（4）make an apology for　　　　　　　　　含义：_____
造句：_____

（5）make up for sth.　　　　　　　　　　　含义：_____
造句：_____

三、客户投诉案例实训

请先进入知识学苑（4-1-3）开展任务实施前的准备，学习客户投诉案例。

知识学苑 (4-1-3)——客户投诉案例

Recently, the customer complaint management department of a freight company receired a complaint from a foreign customer. He said the goods he ordered were damaged in transit more than ten percent of the total price. This is a batch of porcelain used to make tea. The total value is about 50,000 dollars. So, he asked for $5,000 in damages. The customer complaint management department recorded the complaints and verified with the transport department.

After receiving the complaint, the transport department immediately investigated it. They have the following information:

1. Due to the weather, 10% of the goods were damaged in a slight collision.

2. The customer didn't declare the fragile goods and also did not purchase the additional insured service when signing the transportation contract.

According to the contract, the freight company will only be responsible for 10% of the damage, which is 500 dollars. In the process of investigation, we found that the packaging strength of the goods did not fulfill the requirements of fragile articles. Therefore, we suggested that the customer should claim compensation from the seller.

【参考译文】

近日,某货运公司客户投诉管理部接到一位外国客户的投诉。对方称他订购的货物在运输途中损坏了,超过总价的10%。这是一批用来泡茶的瓷器,总价值约5万美元,因此他要求赔偿5 000美元。客户投诉管理部记录下该投诉,并与运输部门核实情况。

运输部门接到投诉后,立即进行了调查。他们了解到以下信息:

(1)由于天气原因,10%的货物在轻微碰撞中受损。

(2)客户在签订运输合同时没有申报易碎品,也没有购买附加保险服务。

根据货运合同,货运公司只承担1%的损失,即500美元。在调查过程中,我们发现货物的包装强度没有达到易碎品的要求。因此,我们建议客户向卖方索赔。

(一) Translate and Record 翻译,并且记录

莎莎从师父王琳积累的投诉案件资料中挑选出一件需要退换货的客户案例,并与小方一起把它翻译成英文,设置为对话练习的情境。

1. Translate

客服:这里是浙江世贸货代公司,有什么可以帮您的?

R: _____

客户:我上次在你们这订购了一批红色的扇子,但是昨天收到的扇子是紫色的。怎么回事?

C: _____

客服:您稍等,我查询下信息。

R: _____

客服:不好意思,可能是配货员疏忽了,目前红色是有货的。

R: _____

客户:我要换货,尽快给我补发。你们这样耽误了我使用,怎么赔偿我的损失?

C: _____

客服:实在很抱歉!我们会尽快安排人员配送,请您将退回的货物交给我们的配送人员。

另外,对于您的损失我们会尽力弥补,请相信我们的诚意。

模块四　售后服务

R: _____

客户：好吧。你们尽快，周五之前一定要送到，否则就没有意义了。

C: _____

客服：我会跟运送部门沟通，尽快给您回复。

R: _____

2. Record

请与同桌练习上述对话，并根据对话内容尝试填写客户投诉信息表，客户信息部分可自行补足，完成表 4-1-1 的填写。

表 4-1-1　客户投诉信息登记表

受理编号				受理日期		
投诉客户				投诉类型		□商品　□服务　□其他
客户地址				联系电话		
投诉理由						
客户要求						
投诉受理	□受理	办理期限			受理人	
	□不受理	理由				
备注						

（二）Act and Practice 根据案例角色扮演，进行对话练习

王琳对莎莎的认真好学很满意，刚好有位老客户打来电话寻求帮助，就打算让莎莎来尝试接手该案件。客户投诉具体信息如下：

受理编号	2020071101		受理日期	7月11日	
投诉客户	上海晶晶食品有限公司		投诉类型		□商品　√服务　□其他
客户地址	上海市××区××路××号		联系电话	138××××××××	
投诉理由	公司购买的 2 台冷链设备出现故障				
客户要求	需要尽快维修				
投诉受理	□受理	办理期限		受理人	
	□不受理	理由			
备注					

（1）如果你是莎莎，请根据提示尝试还原客户诉求并得当回复。

Part A 有礼貌接听，并询问客户诉求。

莎莎：_____

客户：_____

Part B 询问具体情况和相关信息（如产品情况、购买时间、故障原因等）

莎莎：_____

客户：_____

莎莎：_____

客户：_____

Part C 提炼关键信息，判断客户异议类型，并表达服务诚意。

莎莎：_____

客户：_____

莎莎：_____

（2）请与同桌一组，分别扮演上海晶晶食品有限公司的代表和莎莎，根据上述信息设计展开对话练习，可相互交换角色多次练习。

【知识检测】

"认识常见客户异议"这一任务采取自测形式进行评价，请学生在实施任务后对于应掌握的词汇或句型进行回顾，完成 Self-check，对于已掌握的，在它前面的括号中打"√"，完成表 4-1-2 的填写。

模块四 售后服务

表 4-1-2 认识常见客户异议知识自测表

Self-check	
I learned:	
（　）Loss of goods	（　）Goods arrival delay
（　）Return and exchange	（　）Commodity maintenance
（　）I hope you can give me a proper explanation.	
（　）You should have paid for my loss.	
（　）I want to make complaints about your delivery/ marketing.	
（　）The goods I ordered have not been received. What's wrong with it?	
（　）This is not the color I want. I want to exchange it.	
（　）OK. Hold on, please. Let me check the goods' information.	
（　）I have to make an apology for your loss at first.	
（　）Could you tell me the details about that?	
（　）I'm so sorry to hear it, and I need several minutes to ask for information.	
（　）This is a beautiful mistake. We will make up for your loss as soon as possible.	
I can:	
（　）understanding the types of customer complaints .	

Task Two   Communicating Customer Complaint
任务二　沟通客户异议

【任务导入】

莎莎在认识了常见客户异议，并能进行理解、判断和记录后，作为上海前进国际货代公司客服部实习生跟着王琳学习。由于近期客服部的工作量较大，师父希望莎莎能尽快开展实务工作，尤其是针对货物损失和延迟到货这两项最常见的客户异议。

请和莎莎一起完成沟通客户异议的任务吧！

【任务实施】

一、沟通延迟到货类客户异议

请先进入知识学苑（4-1-4）开展任务实施前的准备，学习沟通延迟到货类客户异议的常用句型。

> 知识学苑（4-1-4）——沟通延迟到货类客户异议的常用句型
>
> 在沟通延迟到货类客户异议时，客服人员应虚心接受客户的异议，表达歉意，并向客户解释发生延迟到货的原因，在前期充分询问客户需求的基础上向客户提出解决方案，并再次表达歉意以及希望能继续长期合作的意愿。
>
> （一）虚心接受，表达歉意
> 1. We would like to apologize for the delay in shipping…
> 2. I'm writing to apologize for delaying delivering your…
>
> （二）换位思考，解释原因
> 1. Due to …, it seems impossible for us to process all the cargoes in time.
> 2. We were unable to ship all the goods in time because of…
>
> （三）设身处地，解决问题
> 1. However, we ship your cargo earlier this morning, and we are sure you will receive them by…
> 2. We will send the goods you ordered as soon as possible.
>
> （四）再表歉意，长期合作
> 1. Please accept our sincere apologies again for any inconvenience we have caused you.
> 2. We are sure such delay won't happen again.

（一）Remember and complete 记句型，选择正确词语

在正式沟通前，莎莎认真学习了沟通延迟到货类客户异议的典型句型。下面请从给定的词语中选择正确的单词进行填空。

compensate	compensation	take	make	were expected to	expect to
ruined	loss	see	damage	destroy	apologize	accord to
responsibility	responsible	allow	calculate	inconveniences	bear
apology	according to	precautions	explain	meet	convenience

（1）I'm writing to＿＿＿＿the delay in deliverying＿＿＿＿your cargo.

（2）＿＿＿＿excessive demand last month, it seems＿＿＿＿impossible for us to process all the cargoes＿＿＿＿.

（3）However, we sent your cargo earlier this morning, and we＿＿＿＿you will

receive them by February 17, 2020.

（4）Please accept our sincere_____again for any_____we have caused you.

（5）Thank you very much for your_____.

（6）Yours_____.

（二）Read and Translate 读邮件，翻译沟通邮件

在学习了沟通延迟到货类客户异议的常用句型后，莎莎又从师父王琳处要来了某次与客户大卫沟通异议的邮件，仔细阅读。

请与莎莎一起将英文邮件翻译为中文。

Dear Mr. David,

We would like to apologize for the delay in shipping your cargo.

译文：_____

Due to excessive demand last month, it seems impossible for us to process all the cargoes in time.

译文：_____

However, we sent your cargo earlier this morning, and we are sure you will receive them by February 17, 2020.

译文：_____

Please accept our sincere apologies again for any inconvenience we have caused you.

译文：_____

Thank you very much for your consideration.

译文：_____

Yours truly,

Lin Wang

Shanghai Qianjin International Forwarder Co., Ltd.

译文：_____

（三）Draft and Write 拟提纲，撰写沟通邮件

通过向师父王琳学习，莎莎细致分析了另一位客户彼得的各方面需求，经过仔细查询、认真确认后，拟定了如下沟通客户异议邮件的中文提纲。

1. 拟定沟通客户异议邮件的中文提纲

亲爱的彼得先生：

  对于此次交货延误，我们深表歉意。我们联络的承运人这个月的运输需求过剩，导致甩柜，无法及时处理您的货物。但是，我们已及时催促，将您的货物于今天上午早些时候装运发出了，我们相信您会在 2020 年 5 月 6 日前收到。

  对于由于我们给您带来的不便再次致以真诚的歉意，并非常感谢您的谅解。

  此致

  敬礼

莎莎
上海前进国际货代公司

2. 撰写沟通客户异议英文邮件

二、沟通货物受损类客户异议

请先进入知识学苑（4-1-5）开展任务实施前的准备，学习沟通货物受损类客户异议的常用句型。

知识学苑（4-1-5）——沟通货物受损类客户异议的常用句型

在沟通货物受损类客户异议时，基本沟通原理与沟通延迟交货类客户异议类似。区别在于沟通的事项类别不同，因此，常用句型有所不同。

（一）接纳异议，表态致歉
1. I'm writing to make an apology for the damage of your goods during our transportation.
2. And we will solve the problem promptly.

（二）解释原因，换位思考
1. First please allow me to explain the situation.
2. The goods were expected to arrive 3 days ago, according to our contract. On the way we met with a sudden thunder storm and some of your goods got ruined.
3. The batch of goods indeed arrived on time.
4. So we didn't meet the deadline and have caused certain loss to you.

（三）辨明责任，解决问题
1. It is our company's responsibility for the loss.
2. We announce solemnly that we will bear the burden and compensate for your loss.
3. We will further train our transportation staffs to take precautions before sudden affairs.
4. As for your loss, we will send 2 staff to your company to check your business loss during the past 3 days and calculate the loss amount.
5. We will give you the compensation together with your goods. And we will carry out this job at your convenience, of course.

（四）再表歉意，长期合作
1. Sorry again for the inconveniences we brought to you.
2. Yours sincerely,

（一）Remember and Complete 记句型，选择正确词语

在正式沟通前，莎莎认真学习了沟通货物受损类客户异议的典型句型。下面请从给定的词语中选择正确的单词进行填空。

compensate	compensation	take	make	were expected to	expect to
ruined	loss	see	damage	destroy	apologize	accord to
responsibility	responsible	allow	calculate	inconveniences	bear
apology	according to	precautions	explain	meet	convenience

（1）I'm writing to＿＿＿＿＿ an＿＿＿＿＿ for the＿＿＿＿＿ of your goods during our transportation.

（2）First please＿＿＿＿＿ me to＿＿＿＿＿ the situation.

（3）The goods＿＿＿＿＿ arrive 3 days ago,＿＿＿＿＿ our contract. On the way we met with a sudden thunder storm and some of your goods got＿＿＿＿＿.

（4）So we didn't＿＿＿＿＿ the deadline and have caused certain loss to you.

（5）It is our company's＿＿＿＿＿ for the＿＿＿＿＿.

（6）We announce solemnly that we will＿＿＿＿＿ the burden and＿＿＿＿＿ for your loss.

（7）We will further train our transportation staffs to take＿＿＿＿＿ before sudden affairs.

（8）As for your loss, we will send 2 staff to your company to check your business loss during the past 3 days and＿＿＿＿＿ the loss amount.

（9）We will give you the＿＿＿＿＿ together with your goods. And we will carry out this job at your＿＿＿＿＿.

（10）Sorry again for the＿＿＿＿＿ we brought to you.

（二）Read and Translate 读邮件，翻译沟通邮件

在学习了沟通货物受损类客户异议的常用句型后，莎莎又从师父王琳处要来了某次与客户怀特沟通异议的邮件，仔细阅读。

请与莎莎一起将英文邮件翻译为中文。

Dear Mr. White,
I'm writing to make an apology for the damage of your goods during our transportation.
And we will solve the problem promptly.
译文：＿＿＿＿＿

But first please allow me to explain the situation.
译文：＿＿＿＿＿

You entrusted our company to delivery your goods from Shanghai, China to Jurong, Singapore 15 days ago. And the goods were expected to arrive 3 days ago, according to our contract.
译文：＿＿＿＿＿

But on the way we met with a sudden thunder storm and some of your goods got ruined.
译文：＿＿＿＿＿

模块四 售后服务

The batch of goods indeed arrived on time. But we have to process them for some time. So we didn't meet the deadline and have caused certain loss to you.
译文：_____
_____
_____

It is our company's responsibility for the loss. We announce solemnly that we will bear the burden and compensate for your loss.
译文：_____
_____
_____

And we will further train our transportation staffs to take precautions before sudden affairs.
译文：_____

As for your loss, we will send 2 staff to your company to check your business loss during the past 2 days and calculate the loss amount.
译文：_____
_____
_____

We will give you the compensation together with your goods. And we will carry out this job at your convenience, of course.
译文：_____
_____
_____

Sorry again for the inconveniences we brought to you.
译文：_____
_____
_____

Yours sincerely,
Lin Wang
Shanghai Qianjin International Forwarder Co., Ltd.
译文：_____
_____
_____

（三）Draft and Write 拟提纲，撰写沟通邮件

通过向师父王琳学习，莎莎细致分析了另一位客户文森特（Vincent）的各方面需求，经过仔细查询、认真确认后，拟定了如下沟通客户异议邮件的中文提纲。

1. 拟定沟通客户异议邮件中文提纲

亲爱的文森特先生：

　　您的货物在我公司运输期间产生了货损，因此写这封信向您致歉。我们保证会解决好这个问题的。

　　首先请允许我解释一下情况。十天前，您委托我公司将货物从中国大连运到日本横滨。根据合同，货物三天前就应该到达。由于我们的船只在运输途中突遇暴风雨，您的部分货物也受损了。

　　虽然这批货物准时到达，但是我们必须花费一些时间来处理，以致没有赶上最后期限，给您造成了一定的损失。这是我们公司的责任，我们保证会补偿您的损失。我们将进一步培训我们的运输人员，提高应对突发事件的能力。

　　至于您的损失，我们将派两名员工去贵公司确认在过去三天里您的商业损失金额，我们将在货物到达贵公司后，给予相应的经济补偿。我们会在您方便的时候开展工作。

　　再次对于我们给您带来的不便致以歉意。

　　此致

　　敬礼

莎莎
上海前进国际货代公司

2. 撰写沟通客户异议英文邮件

模块四 售后服务

【知识检测】

"沟通客户异议"这一任务的评价采用自测形式,请学生在实施任务后对于应掌握的词汇或句型进行回顾,完成 Self-check,对于已掌握的,在它前面的括号中打"√",完成表 4-1-3 的填写。

表 4-1-3 沟通客户异议知识自测表

Self-check
I learned:
(　) We would like to apologize for the delay in shipping…
(　) Due to…, it seems impossible for us to process all the cargoes in time.
(　) We were unable to ship all the goods in time because of…
(　) We ship your cargo earlier … and we are sure you will receive them by…
(　) We will send the goods you ordered as soon as possible.
(　) Please accept our sincere apologies again for any inconvenience we have caused you.
(　) We are sure such delay won't happen again.
(　) I'm writing to make an apology for the damage of your goods during our transportation.
(　) And we will solve the problem promptly.
(　) First please allow me to explain the situation.
(　) Goods were expected to arrive 3 days ago, according to our contract. On the way we met with a sudden thunder storm and some of your goods got ruined.
(　) So we didn't meet the deadline and have caused certain loss to you.
(　) We announce solemnly that we will bear the burden and compensate for your loss.
(　) We will further train our transportation staffs to take precautions before sudden affairs.
(　) As for your loss, we will send 2 staff to your company to check your business loss during the past 3 days and calculate the loss amount.
(　) We will give you the compensation together with your goods. And we will carry out this job at your convenience, of course.
(　) Sorry again for the inconveniences we brought to you.
I can:
(　) communicate with customer about goods damage by mail.
(　) communicate with customer about delivery delay by mail.

142

项目二
客户索赔
Project Two Customer Claims

【学习目标】

1. 了解客户投诉、回访和索赔业务流程和范围。
2. 能用流利的英语与客户进行交流,做好售后服务。
3. 在处理投诉与索赔的过程中,树立良好的客户服务意识。

Task One Freight Insurance Premium Inquiry
任务一　询问货运保险费率

【任务导入】

章华是上海前进国际货代公司的实习人员,在他前期联系的客户中有一位与企业长期合作的老客户——艾丽女士,打电话询问章华有关货物运输保险费率的问题。

由于刚进公司不久,章华对国际货代各方面的知识理解较浅显,他担心自己货运保险费率方面的知识掌握得不够扎实,无法解答艾丽女士提出的问题。

请与章华一起认真学习有关货运保险费率的知识吧!

【任务实施】

一、了解货物运输承保范围

请先进入知识学苑(4-2-1)开展任务实施前的学习,认识保险业务中的风险、损失和费用。

> 知识学苑（4-2-1）——认识保险业务中的风险、损失和费用
>
> 1. 风险（Risk）
>   （1）Perils of Sea——海上风险。
>   ① Natural Calamities——自然灾害。
>   ② Fortuitous Accidents——意外事故。
>   （2）Extraneous Risks——外来风险。
> 2. 损失（Average）
>   （1）Total Loss——全部海损。
>   ① Actual Total Loss——实际全损。
>   ② Constructive Total Loss——推定全损。
>   （2）Partial Loss——部分海损。
>   ① General Average，G.A.——共同海损。
>   ② Particular Average，P.A.——单独海损。
> 3. 费用（Cost）
>   （1）Sue and Labour Expenses——施救费用。
>   （2）Salvage Charge——救助费用。

（一）Think and Match 读词汇，匹配风险名称

如图 4-2-1 所示，请将海运风险内容的中文表述与英文表述进行正确连线。

图 4-2-1　海运风险中英文配对

（二）Read and Judge 读对话，判断投保范围

1. Read and Complete The Questions 读下面这段对话，完成下列问题

Ally: Hello, I have a shipment to Australia for your company. I'd like to inquire about insurance.

Zhang Hua: Okay, what can I do for you?

Ally: Due to the special nature of the goods, we would like to insure it, and would like to know, what risks can be taken from the Insurance Company?

Zhang Hua: In the insurance business, there are three basic concepts: risk, average and cost. When the goods occur perils of sea and extraneous risks, can be insured.

Ally: What are the perils of sea?

Zhang Hua: Perils of sea include two aspects: natural calamities and fortuitous accidents. Such as: bad weather, lightning, tsunamis, earthquakes, floods or volcanic eruptions and other human force majeure disasters.

Ally: Is grounding, sinking, collision insurable?

Zhang Hua: These are the fortuitous accidents mentioned above and are insurable.

Ally: Well, I understand the risks at sea, but what about the extraneous risks?

Zhang Hua: Extraneous risks refers to the loss caused by theft, shortage, rain, defilement, leakage, breakage, damp, heat, smell, rust, hook damage, war, strike, etc.

Ally: Oh, I understand. Thank you!

Zhang Hua: My pleasure.

（1）What are the three aspects of risk? 风险包括哪三方面？

a）＿＿＿＿＿＿＿＿＿＿＿＿＿＿＿＿

b）＿＿＿＿＿＿＿＿＿＿＿＿＿＿＿＿

c）＿＿＿＿＿＿＿＿＿＿＿＿＿＿＿＿

（2）Risk classification. 风险分类

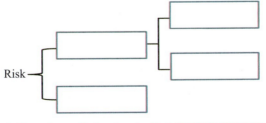

2. Find out what the following risks include 下面这些风险包括哪些内容

（1）Natural Calamities contains：

模块四 售后服务

（2）Fortuitous Accidents contains：

（3）Extraneous Risks contains：

二、明确货物运输保险险别

在了解了保险业务涉及的内容后，还需要对保险险别有所了解，请进入知识学苑（4-2-2）开展任务实施前的学习。常见的货物运输保险分为基本险（China Insurance Clause, C.I.C.）和附加险（Additional risk）两大类。

知识学苑（4-2-2）——常见的货物运输保险险别

1. 基本险
①平安险（Free from Particular Clause, F.P.A.）。
②水渍险（With Particular Average, W.P.A.）。
③一切险（All Risks, A.R.）。

2. 附加险
附加险有两大类：一类是一般附加险，另一类是特殊附加险。
（1）一般附加险（11种）。
①偷窃、提货不着险（Thief, Pilferage and Non Delivery）。
②淡水雨淋险（Fresh Water and Rain Damage）。
③短量险（Risk of Shortage）。
④混杂、玷污险（Intermixture and Contamination）。
⑤渗漏险（Leakage）。
⑥碰损破碎险（Clashing and Breakage Risk）。
⑦串味险（Risk of Odour）。
⑧受潮受热险（Sweating and Heating Risk）。
⑨钩损险（Hook Damage）。
⑩包装破裂险（Loss for Damage Caused by Breakage of Packing）。
⑪锈损险（Risk of Rust）。
（2）特殊附加险（8种）。
①交货不到险（Failure to Delivery Risk）。
②进口关税险（Import Duty Risk）。
③舱面险（On Deck Risk）。
④拒收险（Rejection Risk）。
⑤黄曲霉素险（Aflatoxin Risk）。
⑥出口货物到香港或澳门存仓火险责任扩张条款（Fire Risk Extension Clause for Storage of Cargo at Destination Hong Kong Including Kowloon or Macao）。
⑦罢工险（Strikes Risk）。
⑧战争险（War Risks）。

（一）Think and Match 读词汇，匹配险别名称

在"知识学苑"中学习了常见海运保险险别后，章华认识了不少保险种类，他尝试

将每项常见海运保险险别的英文全称或英文缩写与它的中文名称匹配起来。

如图 4-2-2 所示,请将海运保险险别的英文表述与中文表述进行正确连线。

图 4-2-2　常见海运保险险别中英文配对

(二) Reading Comprehension 阅读理解

认识了货物运输保险险别的中英文表述后,仅凭这些知识章华仍不能完成解答客户问题的任务,请阅读下文,帮助章华找出文中提及的保险险别,判断保险业务涉及的承保范围,加深对各种货物运输保险的认识。

1. Read

People's Insurance Company of China (PICC), a Chinese insurance company. The insurance in PICC (2009) is classified into three conditions: Free from Particular Average (FPA), With Particular Average (WPA) and All Risks.

a) Free from Particular Average(FPA)

Total or constructive total loss of the whole consignment of cargo caused in the course of transit by natural casualties such as heavy weather, lightning, tsunami, earthquake and flood.

Total loss or partial loss incurred as a result of fortuitous accidents such as collision, stranding, sinking of the vessel, in collision with floating ice or other objects and fire or explosion.

模块四　售后服务

General average and salvage charges, reasonable costs incurred by the assured in salvaging the goods or averting or minimizing a loss recoverable under the policy.

Losses attributable to discharge of the insured goods at a port of distress following a sea peril as well special charges arising from loading, warehousing and forwarding of the goods at an intermediate port of caller refuge.

b) With Particular Average (WPA)

Aside from the risks covered under FPA condition as above, WPA also covers partial loss and damage is recoverable from the insurer resulting from natural calamities.

c) All Risks

Aside from the risks covered under the FPA and WPA/WA conditions as above, it also provides insurance against all risks of loss of or damage to the insured goods arising from general external causes in the course of transit. The general additional risks are as follows: theft, pilferage&non delivery risks, fresh water and/or rain damage risks, shortage risks, intermixture and contamination risks, leakage risks, clash and breakage risks, taint of odor risks, sweat and heating risks, hook damage risks, breakage of packing risks and rust risks. The All Risks does not cover special additional risks such as risks of war, strike, failure to delivery, import duty, on deck, rejection, aflatoxin etc.

【参考译文】

中国人民保险公司是一家中国保险公司。中国人民保险公司（2009年）的保险分为三种情况：平安险、水渍险和一切险。

a）平安险

因恶劣天气、雷电、海啸、地震、洪水等自然灾害在运输途中造成的全部或者推定全部货物损失。

因船舶碰撞、搁浅、沉没、与浮冰或者其他物体相撞、起火、爆炸等偶然事故造成的全部或者部分损失。

共同海损和救助费用，被保险人为救助货物或者避免或者尽量减少保险单规定的可赔偿损失而发生的合理费用。

海难发生后，被保险货物在危难港卸货所造成的损失，以及货物在保险港中途装卸、仓储和运输所产生的特别费用。

b）水渍险

除上述平安险外，水渍险亦包括部分损失，而损失可向保险人追讨。

c）一切险

除了上述平安险和水渍险条件所保的险别外，一切险别还包括在运输途中由一般外部原因引起的被保险货物的全部或部分灭失或损坏的一切险别。一般附加险包括：盗窃险、偷窃险和未交货险、淡水险和／或雨水险、缺货险、混合险和污染险、渗漏险、碰撞险和破损险、臭味险、汗水险和热风险、钩损险、包装破损险和锈蚀险。一切险不包括特殊附加险，如战争险、罢工险、未交货险、进口税、甲板险、拒收险、黄曲霉毒素险等。

2. Read and Choose 阅读并选出正确答案

a）What are the two main types of cargo transportation insurance?
货物运输保险主要分为哪两大类？

☐（1）Free from Particular Clause (F.P.A.).
☐（2）China Insurance Clause (C.I.C.).
☐（3）Additional Risk.
☐（4）War Risks.

b）What kinds of insurance cover are mentioned in the passage? 文章中提到了哪些保险，请找出来，并将保险险别的中英文写在横线上。

（1）_____   （2）_____
（3）_____   （4）_____
（5）_____   （6）_____
（7）_____   （8）_____
（9）_____   （10）_____
（11）_____ （12）_____

c）All risks also include special additional risks, such as war risk, strike risk, non-delivery risk, import duty, deck risk, non-collection risk, aflatoxins risk, etc. 一切险还包括特殊附加险，如战争险、罢工险、不交货险、进口关税险、甲板险、不收货险、黄曲霉毒素险等。

☐ Right
☐ Wrong

三、沟通保险问题

章华已经掌握了初级货运保险知识，要想得到进一步提升，并顺利与客户沟通，还需要对知识学苑（4-2-3）进行学习，掌握回答客户询问保险保费问题时的典型语句。

模块四 售后服务

知识学苑（4-2-3）——回答保险保费问询时的典型句型

询问保险保费既要明确说明保险险别又要确定保费的报价数值，也要注意用好礼貌用语，关注客户的感受，典型句型如下。

1. Please insure FPA on your side.

译文：请在您那边投保平安险。

2. We have insured the goods against All Risks.

译文：我们已为货物投保了一切险。

3. We will effect insurance on your behalf.

译文：我们愿代你方投保。

4. The seller shall insure against all risks with the People's insurance company of China for 110% of the invoice value.

译文：由卖方按发票金额的110%向中国人民保险公司投保一切险。

5. If any damage to the goods occurs a claim may be filled with the insurance agent at your end, who will undertake to compensate for the loss sustained.

译文：货物如发生损坏，可向贵地的保险代理提出索赔，他们将赔偿你方遭受的损失。

6. Enclosed please find the inspection certificate issued by the Beijing Inspection and Quarantine Bureau, the shipping agent's certificate and the original insurance policy.

译文：随函附上北京检验检疫局出具的检验证明、船务代理人的证明以及保险单原件。

7. Insurance claims should be filed with the insurance company or its agent within 30 days after the arrival of the goods at the port of destination.

译文：应在货物抵达目的港后30天内向保险公司或其代理人提出保险索赔。

通过以上学习，章华大致了解了保险及保险费率的相关知识，但还是感到心中没底，忐忑不安，货代员老李为帮助章华树立信心，给他出了一些题目，希望他可以从中体会如何解答客户的问询。

（一）Translate 中英文互译

1. English to Chinese

a）Please insure A.R. at your end.

译文：_____

b）We have insured the goods against Risk of Shortage.

译文：_____

c）We have arranged the necessary Insurance effected cover.

译文：_____

d）Insurance on the goods shall be covered by us for 110%. of the CIF value.

译文：_____

e) Insurance claims should be filed with the insurance company or its agent within 60 days after the arrival of the goods at the port of destination.

译文：_____

2. Chinese to English

a）请在您那边投保水渍险。

译文：_____

b）这份保单给我们保了破碎险。

译文：_____

c）由卖方按发票金额的110%向中国人民保险公司投保平安险。

译文：_____

d）保险金额为发票金额的110%，直至目的港为止。

译文：_____

（二）Read and Answer 朗读对话并回答有关小题

请与同桌练习这一通电话，加深保费咨询的相关内容，学会如何与客户就保费问题进行沟通。

Ally: I'm calling to discuss the insurance coverage for the order you requested.

Zhang Hua: We have pleasure in informing that shipment of your Order No. 23545 covers 10 metric tons of Small Red Beans. What kind of insurance do you need?

Ally: Please insure All Risks on your side. And we would feel more comfortable with the additional protection.

Zhang Hua: The All Risks does not cover special additional risks such as risks of war, strike, failure to delivery, import duty, on deck, rejection, aflatoxin etc. Do you require Additional risk?

Ally: What's the rate?

Zhang Hua: I believe that we have requested an amount twenty-five percent above the invoice value?

Ally: We think it's a little excessive.

Zhang Hua: I can understand your concern. However, the normal coverage for goods

of this type is to insure them for the total invoice amount plus ten percent.

Ally: I see.

Zhang Hua: If you want to increase the coverage, we will have to charge you extra for the additional cost.

Ally: But the insurance was supposed to be included in the quotation.

Zhang Hua: Yes, but we quoted you normal coverage at regular rates. If you need, we will effect insurance on your behalf.

Ally: Fax me whatever rates you find there and I'll compare them with what we can offer.

Zhang Hua: Yeah, sure. No problem.

（1）根据自身情况，将有疑问或不确定的单词摘抄下来，着重理解。

a）

b）

c）

d）

e）

（2）Please consider and answer what are the additional risks？请思考并回答文中加粗字体部分的问题，即附加险有哪些？

【知识检测】

"询问货运保险费率"这一任务的评价采用自测形式，请学生在实施任务后对于应掌握的词汇或句型进行回顾，完成Self-check，对于已掌握的，在它前面的括号中打"√"，完成表4-2-1的填写。

表 4-2-1　询问货运保险费率知识自测表

Self-check				
I learned:				
（　）F.P.A.	（　）W.P.A.		（　）War Risks	（　）Clashing and Breakage Risk
（　）A.R.	（　）Risks		（　）Strikes Risk	（　）Indemnify
（　）G.A.	（　）P.A.		（　）People's Insurance Company of China	
（　）Total or constructive total loss of the whole consignment of cargo caused in the course of transit by natural casualties such as heavy weather, lightning, tsunami, earthquake and flood.				
（　）Total loss or partial loss incurred as a result of fortuitous accidents such as collision, stranding, sinking of the vessel, in collision with floating ice or other objects and fire or explosion.				
（　）General average and salvage charges, reasonable costs incurred by the assured in salvaging the goods or averting or minimizing a loss recoverable under the policy.				
（　）Insurance on the goods shall be shouldered by ... for 110%. of the CIF value.				
（　）Regarding insurance, the Insured amount is for 110% of invoice value up to				
（　）This policy covers us against ...				
（　）We shall cover ... and ... as usual				
（　）In accordance with your request, we shall insure the goods for 110% of the invoice value.				
I can:				
（　）make premium quotation by telephone.				

Task Two　Communicating insurance claims
任务二　沟通保险索赔

【任务导入】

客户索赔是货代公司一定会遇到的问题，可能是因为运输途中包装破损或者货物破损而导致的索赔，可能是一些不可控或不可抗拒因素导致的索赔，很多人收到客户投诉后便急得像热锅上的蚂蚁，章华也一样。

模块四 售后服务

当章华收到客户投诉后想马上给客户回复邮件时，老李制止了章华，他建议章华解读完以下内容，然后再考虑回复客户的邮件。

请与章华一起学习有关保险索赔的技巧与禁忌并完成沟通任务！

【任务实施】

一、索赔内容

请先进入知识学苑 (4-2-4) 开展任务实施前的学习，了解异议和索赔条款内容。

知识学苑 (4-2-4)——异议与索赔条款内容

1. 索赔依据（Basis of claim）
索赔依据包括法律依据（Legal Basis）和事实依据（Factual Basis）
2. 索赔期限（Time limit for claim）
① ×× days after the goods reach the destination——货物达到目的地后 ×× 天起算
② ×× days after discharge of cargo from seagoing vessel at the port of destination——货物到达目的港卸离海轮后 ×× 天起算
③ ×× days after the arrival of the goods at the seller's place of business or the user's place of business——货物到达卖方营业处所或用户所在地后 ×× 天起算
④ Counting from ×× days after the goods are re-inspected——货物复验后 ×× 天起算
3. 索赔办法（Claim method）
异议索赔条款对合同双方当事人都有约束力，不论何方违约，受损害方都有权利提出索赔。鉴于索赔是一项复杂而又重要的工作，故处理索赔时，应弄清事实，分清责任，并区别不同情况，有理有据地提出索赔。

填空

1. Complete

a) Content of objection and claim clause includes＿＿＿＿and＿＿＿＿.

b) The Basis of claim includes＿＿＿＿and＿＿＿＿.

c) Time limit for claim is ×× days after ＿＿＿＿.

d) Time limit for claim is ×× days after ＿＿＿＿.

e) Time limit for claim is ×× days after ＿＿＿＿.

2. Translation

a) 货物达到目的地后 ×× 天起算。

译文：＿＿＿＿

b) 货物到达目的港卸离海轮后 ×× 天起算。

译文：＿＿＿＿

a）货物到达卖方营业处所或用户所在地后××天起算。

译文：_____.

b）货物复验后××天起算。

译文：_____.

二、面对索赔，如何与客户沟通

在与客户沟通时，只明确索赔内容是远远不够的，请再进入知识学苑(4-2-5)和(4-2-6)学习与赔偿相关的英语术语。

知识学苑 (4-2-5)——常见赔偿术语

to approach .... For compensation——向……要求赔偿
to lodge/make/raise/issue/file/register/put in/ bring up a claim——提出索赔
claim on goods——就货物索赔
claim for damage——就损坏索赔
claim for amount——就数量索赔
claim with/against somebody——向某人索赔
to accept a claim——接受索赔
to entertain a claim——受理索赔
to admit a claim——同意索赔
to dismiss a claim——驳回索赔
to reject/decline/turn down a claim——拒绝索赔
to settle a claim——解决索赔
to waive a claim——放弃索赔
to withdraw a claim——撤回索赔
be prompt and equitable in settling claims——理赔方面公平合理

知识学苑 (4-2-6)——常见索赔沟通句型

If you have any questions, please feel free to contact me directly. We'll take care of it and be responsible.

如果您有任何问题，请直接联系我。我们会处理好并负责任的。

Hello, please forgive me if I have offended you, because it is not what you think.

您好，如果我冒犯了您，请原谅我，但是这个问题的原因并不是您想的那样。

This problem is caused by ...., I hope you can understand it. If you still have any questions, please feel free to contact me directly.

这个问题是由……引起的，我希望您能理解，如果您还有异议，您也可以直接联系我。

Hello, I have already explained our judgment and plan. We considered the plan carefully. We are very sorry we can't satisfy you. We hope that you can understand us.

您好，我已经解释了我们的判断意见和处理方案，这已经是我们仔细考虑过的方案，很抱歉不能满足你的所有要求，希望您能理解。

（一）Think and Match 读词汇，匹配常用赔偿术语

如图 4-2-3 所示，请将常见赔偿术语的中文表述与英文表述进行正确连线。

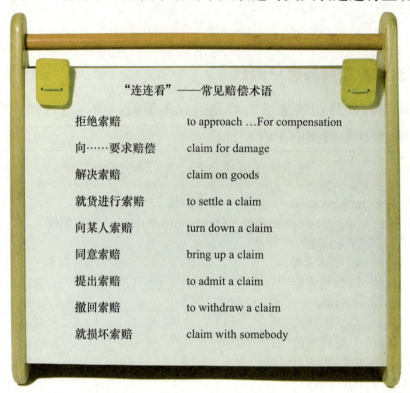

图 4-2-3　常见赔偿术语中英文配对

（二）Answer the Questions as Requested 按要求回答问题

面对索赔，首先应该对客户表示完全理解，如果是自己方面的错误，要立即道歉，如果需要调查情况，跟客户说已上报领导，然后尽快组织开会，调查事情经过。

解决索赔的步骤如下：

1. Please answer the questions in English

Steps to resolve a claim is:

(1) _____

(2) _____

(3) _____

2. How to say?

(1) When a client asks who caused the problem　当客户问起问题是谁造成的时

You could say:_____

(2) When the customer is not satisfied with the solution　当客户不满意解决方案时

You could say:＿＿＿＿＿＿＿＿＿＿＿＿＿＿＿＿＿＿＿＿＿＿＿＿＿＿＿＿＿＿＿＿

(3) When a client suspects you　当客户怀疑你时

You can say:＿＿＿＿＿＿＿＿＿＿＿＿＿＿＿＿＿＿＿＿＿＿＿＿＿＿＿＿＿＿＿＿＿

3. Chinese to English

a) This problem you find ... to deal with, this is his jurisdiction.

译文：＿＿＿＿＿＿＿＿＿＿＿＿＿＿＿＿＿＿＿＿＿＿＿＿＿＿＿＿＿＿＿＿＿＿

b) That's the way it's gonna be. You got a problem with that, you take it up with ...

译文：＿＿＿＿＿＿＿＿＿＿＿＿＿＿＿＿＿＿＿＿＿＿＿＿＿＿＿＿＿＿＿＿＿＿

c) Hello, please forgive me if I have offended you verbally, because it is / not what you think.

译文：＿＿＿＿＿＿＿＿＿＿＿＿＿＿＿＿＿＿＿＿＿＿＿＿＿＿＿＿＿＿＿＿＿＿

d) If you have any questions, please feel free to contact me directly.

译文：＿＿＿＿＿＿＿＿＿＿＿＿＿＿＿＿＿＿＿＿＿＿＿＿＿＿＿＿＿＿＿＿＿＿

三、回复客户索赔邮件

收到客户邮件，首先应该回复并安抚客户，告诉他不要着急，并要求客户提供具体的卸货前照片或视频，或者第三方质检报告，同时要与自己公司部门比对记录，研究具体的问题根源以及具体的解决方案，然后给客户一个明确的说法，再进一步与客户协商可接受的解决方案。

（一）Read and Translate 阅读并翻译

请阅读该邮件，理解邮件内容，学习邮件格式，将邮件翻译成中文。

1.Read

Dear Andy,

Could you provide us with the pictures or videos or any Third Party Inspection Reports of the items with problems?

On that condition, we'll be able to check with our...&..., so we can get this problem clearly and provide you with possible practical solutions.

Wait for your positive feedback soon.（Call-To-Action）

Warm Regards,

Michael

模块四　售后服务

2. Translate

译文：_____
_____
_____
_____

（二）Write and Remember 摘抄并记忆

对于投诉与索赔事宜，章华认认真真学习完老李给的资料后，觉得更有把握与信心了。他想将自己的知识储备得更充分些，于是章华利用网络工具，查找了一系列关于回答投诉与索赔的话术并记录下来。

1. _____
2. _____
3. _____
4. _____
5. _____

（三）Read and Write 阅读并撰写

Urgent Help: An old customer, after receiving the goods found damaged, claim. Based on the circumstances of the loss: 2,600 pounds for packing and 1,000 cases of unsalable goods, the claim amount is awarded at 11,350 pounds and it is hoped that it will be settled as soon as possible.

（1）根据上述情况，从索赔依据入手，请客户提供关于破损的图片与证明。

Given the circumstances of this appeal, please.
_____
_____

（2）结合1中建议，请你协助章华给客户回复一封邮件，说明赔偿事宜。

Dear ×××,

Thanks for your email. I fully understand your situation. I'm sorry to hear that
_____
_____
_____
_____

Best regards,

×××

【知识检测】

保险索赔沟通这一任务的评价采用自测形式，请学生在实施任务后对于应掌握的词汇或句型进行回顾，完成 Self-check，对于已掌握的，在它前面的括号中打"√"，完成表 4-2-2 的填写。

表 4-2-2　保险索赔知识自测表

Self-check	
I learned:	
（　）basis of claim	（　）legal Basis
（　）factual basis	（　）time limit for claim
（　）Claim method	（　）claim for amount
（　）claim on goods	（　）to accept a claim
（　）turn down a claim	（　）to settle a claim
（　）to waive a claim	（　）be prompt and equitable in settling claims
（　）If you have any questions, please feel free to contact me directly.	
（　）Hello, please forgive me if I have offended you, because it's not what you think.	
（　）This problem is caused by ..., I hope you can understand. If you still have objections, you can also carry out more consultation and verification.	
（　）Hello, I have already explained our judgment opinion and the processing plan, this already was the plan which we carefully considered, very sorry, can not satisfy your all requirements, hoped that you can understand.	
I can:	
（　）answer e-mails to clients.	